China: Violations of Human Rights

*Prisoners of conscience and the
death penalty in the
People's Republic of China*

Amnesty International Publications

First published 1984 by Amnesty International Publications
1 Easton Street, London WC1X 8DJ, United Kingdom

Copyright © 1984 Amnesty International Publications

ISBN 0-939994-10-0
AI Index: ASA 17/11/84
Original Language: English

Printed in the United States of America

The following photographs are copyright: pages 7, 8, 12, 13 © Gamma Press.

Contents

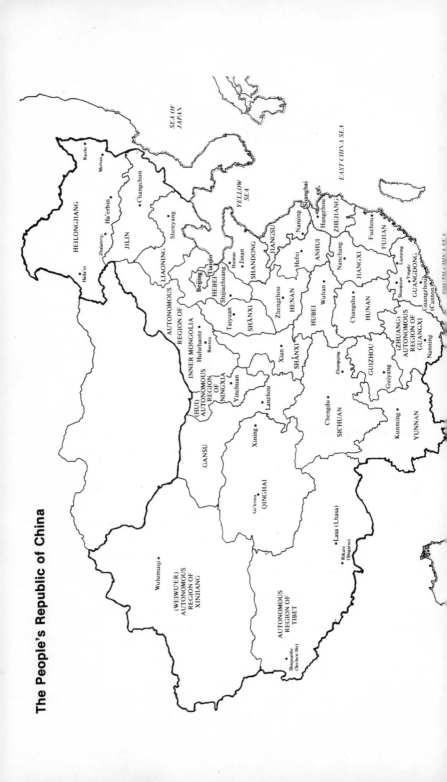

The People's Republic of China

Introduction

Amnesty International's concerns in the People's Republic of China include:

— the arrest and imprisonment of prisoners of conscience and the existence of legislation providing for their detention;

— the prolonged detention without trial of people arrested on political grounds;

— inadequate trial procedures and the absence of legal safeguards to assure fair and open trials for people arrested on political grounds;

— the reported ill-treatment of prisoners, usually in detention centres administered by Public Security Bureaus, and conditions of detention;

— the extensive use of the death penalty.

Most of these concerns are long-standing and have continued despite major legislative changes in 1979: they were addressed by Amnesty International in November 1978 in a report on political imprisonment in the People's Republic of China.

Amnesty International has communicated its concerns to the Chinese Government on numerous occasions, both in writing and through discussions held in New York and Geneva in the past two years between representatives of the People's Republic of China and of Amnesty International.

On 28 February 1983 the organization submitted a memorandum to the Government of the People's Republic of China describing its concerns in detail and outlining Amnesty International's mandate and working methods. It explained that under its mandate Amnesty International works for the release of prisoners of conscience, that is, people detained for exercising their fundamental human rights who have not used or advocated violence. The organization also seeks to ensure that all political prisoners are charged and tried within a reasonable time and that any trial procedures relating to such prisoners conform to internationally recognized norms. The term "political prisoner" as used by Amnesty International refers to anyone who is imprisoned, detained or otherwise physically restricted where the motivation of the authorities or of the prisoner appears to be political. Amnesty International also opposes the imposition of the death penalty and the torture or cruel, inhuman or degrading treatment of all prisoners. Together with the memorandum Amnesty International submitted a list of people it considered to be prisoners of conscience and of people reportedly held on political grounds about whom it lacked detailed information. It asked the government to provide information on all the prisoners listed. In an accompanying letter to Premier Zhao Ziyang, Amnesty International invited the comments of the government on the memorandum and said it would value an opportunity to discuss them with an appropriate representative. By the end of 1983, however, Amnesty International had received no response. In another letter addressed to Premier Zhao Ziyang in January 1984 Amnesty International reiterated its interest in receiving comments from the government on the memorandum. It also raised its concerns over new arrests, the trials of prisoners of conscience which had taken place since the submission of the memorandum, and the extensive use of the death penalty from August 1983.

On 2 May 1984 Amnesty International informed the government of its intention to publish the memorandum, saying that it would publish with it any reply from the government that reached it before the beginning of June. No comments or response from the government were received by that date.

In addition to making public this memorandum, the present report includes a chapter on prisoners of conscience and one on the death penalty.

Since the submission of the memorandum Amnesty International's concerns about the imprisonment of prisoners of conscience, about judicial procedures relating to political prisoners and about conditions of detention have continued. Two prisoners of conscience mentioned in the memorandum—Ren Wanding and Chen Lu—are reported to have been released since the document was presented to the government. However, others referred to in the memorandum are still in detention and there have been further arrests. Some prisoners of conscience adopted by Amnesty International have been tried during 1983 in closed trials that fell short of international standards. The first part of this report addresses these concerns and includes illustrative cases of people currently in detention believed by Amnesty International to be prisoners of conscience.

Another major concern of Amnesty International since the submission of the memorandum has been the extensive use of the death penalty since the start of a "campaign against crime" in August 1983. During this campaign legislation was adopted which removed vital safeguards in order to accelerate the procedures for trial, appeal and execution in some death penalty cases. These changes and their effects are described in the second part of this report.

The memorandum published in the third chapter of this report is the main text of the document submitted by Amnesty International to the Government of the People's Republic of China in February 1983. The list of prisoners which had been attached as an appendix to the memorandum, and the introduction, which mainly gave an explanation of Amnesty International's mandate and methods of work, have not been included. Amnesty International's concerns with regard to human rights violations in the People's Republic of China, as listed earlier, are addressed in some detail in the five sections of the memorandum. The final section of the memorandum consists of conclusions and recommendations addressed by Amnesty International to the Government of the People's Republic of China. In the introduction, the organization had called upon the government to consider the implementation of these recommendations.

Prisoners of conscience

Amnesty International's information on the detention of prisoners of conscience in China remains incomplete; little official information about prisoners is published and the authorities have not usually replied to Amnesty International's inquiries about individual cases. Amnesty International believes that the prisoners of conscience of whom it is aware are only a small fraction of the total number in the People's Republic of China.

Official Chinese sources occasionally provide information which gives some indication of the scale of political imprisonment in China. "Counter-revolutionary" cases accounted for "only 0.5 per cent of the total of criminal cases" tried by the courts in 1982, according to a report by the President of the Supreme People's Court in June 1983. Citing "incomplete statistics", the official weekly *Beijing Review* of 6 June 1983 also said that lawyers acting for the defence in criminal cases had "handled more than 90,000 criminal cases in 1982". These figures indicate a minimum of 450 "counter-revolutionary" cases tried by the courts in 1982. In addition an unknown number of political prisoners were detained without trial by being assigned to "re-education through labour" camps or were awaiting trial. The total number of people arrested and held on criminal charges but not yet tried throughout the country in 1982 was officially put at 748,000 (New China News Agency, 12 June 1983).

In early 1983 the prison director of Shanghai's main prison told a foreign journalist that two per cent of the prisoners held there were "counter-revolutionaries". According to him, the prison housed 3,500 male and female prisoners. Similar proportions have occasionally been mentioned by officials of other penal institutions. Officials of Beijing Prison No. 1 interviewed by foreign visitors in 1981 and 1982 said that three per cent of the 1,900 prisoners held there had committed "counter-revolutionary" crimes. In addition to convicted prisoners, such as those held in these two prisons, untried political prisoners are also held in detention centres and in labour camps.

According to former prisoners, most penal institutions hold political prisoners, either convicted or untried. All large and medium-sized cities have a number of prisons, detention centres and labour camps. Beijing municipality, for instance, has four prisons, including Beijing Prison No. 1; three main detention centres administered by the municipal Public Security Bureau (police); and five detention centres administered by the Public Security Sub-Bureaux of the five city districts. It also controls several labour camps with a capacity varying from about 1,000 prisoners in the smallest camps to over 20,000 in the largest. Each province also has a network of labour camps and some particularly large complexes of corrective labour farms and camps are reported to exist in remote provinces, such as Qinghai, Xinjiang, Tibet and provinces in the northeast of the country.

Although little official information is available about the number of political prisoners currently held, some indication of the number detained on political grounds or deprived of their rights in the late 1960s and 1970s has been given in the past few years. An extensive review was undertaken in the late 1970s to correct miscarriages of justice committed during the Cultural Revolution (1966-1976) and the previous decade. Official sources have reported that this led to the rehabilitation of several million people who had been deprived of their rights, detained or punished in other ways. In addition, some 1,200,000 cases which came to trial during the Cultural Revolution in which people were formally sentenced to imprisonment or other punishments had been re-examined by the courts by the end of 1981. Over 300,000 of these were declared to have been "unjust", "frame-ups" or "wrong". Officials of Beijing Prison No. 1 contrasted the number of political prisoners currently held—three per cent—with 40 per cent in 1965 and as many as 70 per cent during the following decade (1966-1976), in interviews in 1981 and 1982.

The number of political prisoners may be small compared with the past, but arrests have continued since the large-scale rehabilitation of the late 1970s, and it remains difficult, indeed impossible, for Amnesty International to estimate the total number of prisoners of conscience.

Legislation

Since 1979 the People's Republic of China has adopted a number of laws in an effort both to build up the legal system and to put an end to the "lawlessness" which had prevailed during the Cultural Revolution. Some fundamental legislation was adopted which had previously been non-existent. Most important of the new laws relevant to political imprisonment were the Criminal Law and the

Law of Criminal Procedure. Both were adopted in July 1979 and came into force in January 1980. Drafted during a period of "liberalization", the new legislation provides in principle greater protection for individual rights than previous legislation. For instance it increased guarantees of the rights of the defence and provided more safeguards against arbitrary detention.

The "democracy wall" in Beijing (Peking). This is where wall-posters calling for democratic reforms and respect for human rights were posted during the "democracy movement" that started in the Chinese capital in late 1978 and soon spread to the other main cities.

However, the new laws also contain provisions which can be used to imprison people for the peaceful exercise of fundamental human rights. Most of these provisions are included in a section of the Criminal Law dealing with "counter-revolutionary" offences. In particular, Articles 98 and 102 of the Criminal Law provide for people found guilty of the following offences to be imprisoned: "counter-revolutionary propaganda and agitation"; organizing or taking part in a "counter-revolutionary group"; and incitement "to resist arrest or violate the law and statutes of the State". People detained for expressing their opinions or exercising peacefully other basic rights in the past few years have most often been charged under these articles. Other prisoners of conscience were convicted under other articles of the Criminal Law which refer to "endangering the sovereignty and security of the motherland" and "supplying information to the enemy".

Shortly after the new legislation had been adopted the first political trial to receive publicity in the Chinese media since the Cultural

Revolution took place in Beijing. Wei Jingsheng, the young editor of an unofficial journal, was detained on account of his outspoken comments on Chinese political affairs. His case is described in the following pages. His trial generated a large number of articles in the official press, including comments by Chinese legal experts on

The trial of prisoner of conscience Wei Jingsheng: the trial that marked the end of the period of "liberalization" that had begun in 1978 and that had seen the emergence of the "democracy movement". Prisoners usually have their heads shaved if they are convicted of a crime. Wei Jingsheng's head has already been shaved—before the outcome of his trial. He was sentenced to 15 years' imprisonment on 16 October 1979 for "counter-revolutionary crimes". In the photograph a public security agent shows Wei a copy of the unofficial journal *Exploration*, in which he had published articles criticizing aspects of official policies.

the "legal limits" of free speech. The New China News Agency reported, for instance, on 10 November 1979 that Wu Wenzao, the Vice-President of Beijing High People's Court, had indicated that people with dissenting views could not be prosecuted "unless they spread their views in jeopardy of society". Another jurist, Rui Mu (of the Legal Commission of the National People's Congress) stated that "in any country" the freedoms guaranteed in the constitution had their legal limits: they may not "jeopardise national security and social order—and these two restrictions are subject to interpretations of the ruling class according to its own interests". The *People's Daily* of 17 October 1979 also published the following warning to people who "for a period of time" had tried to defend Wei Jingsheng and who shared his views:

"We want to advise these people: Your calculations are wrong. You had better stop daydreaming. (. . .)

"Regardless of the banners of so-called human rights, democracy and what not flaunted by Wei Jingsheng, and regardless of who openly tried to defend him, because of the irrefutable evidence of his counter-revolutionary crimes, he must be punished according to the law.

"Here we also want to advise those people who were fooled and deceived fully to understand: Socialist democracy must be developed, and the socialist legal system must be strengthened. But anyone who actually engages in counter-revolutionary activities in the name of democracy must know that the people of the whole country will not allow it."

According to unofficial sources the trial of Wei Jingsheng and the attendant publicity in the official press was meant as a warning to other young activists who openly and critically discussed political affairs. It indicated generally the limits of the reforms brought about by the new legislation.

In November 1979, shortly after Wei Jingsheng's trial, a law permitting detention without charge or trial which had been adopted in 1957* was revived by the Standing Committee of the National People's Congress (China's parliament) when supplementary regulations were adopted. This law institutes administrative detention for people considered to have "anti-socialist views" or to be "hooligans", for the purpose of "re-educating them through labour". They can be detained for up to four years on simple police order, without being charged or having access to any judicial process. Special labour camps exist for those held under this legislation.**

In addition to including provisions which have been used to imprison people for the non-violent exercise of basic rights, the new laws adopted in 1979 also fail to guarantee some of the minimum safeguards spelled out in international human rights conventions. They give insufficient protection against arbitrary arrest and fail to guarantee a fair trial. For example, they do not guarantee the right to receive visits from relatives and legal counsel shortly after arrest and regularly thereafter, the right to adequate time and facilities

---

* Its title is "Decision of the State Council of the People's Republic of China on the Question of Rehabilitation Through Labour", 1957. See Memorandum to the Government of the People's Republic of China for further details.

** They are commonly known as "labour re-education" *(laojiao)* prisoners, by contrast to convicted prisoners who are known as "labour-reform" prisoners *(laogai)*.

for preparation of the defence, and the right to be presumed innocent until proved guilty in a court of law.

Amnesty International has been concerned also that certain rights which are guaranteed by the new legislation have been violated in a number of cases. In particular, certain provisions on arrest and detention and on the right to public trial have not been followed. According to the law, for instance, a person is formally "arrested" only when charges are brought against him or her and preliminary detention should not last more than six days, or a maximum of 10 days in "special cases" (Arrest and Detention Act of the PRC, 1979, Article 8). Furthermore, within 24 hours of detention the family of the person concerned should be notified of the reason and the place of detention (Arrest and Detention Act of the PRC, Article 5). However, in the cases of many prisoners of conscience known to Amnesty International, these provisions were violated and prisoners were not allowed to see their relatives for long periods of time. For example, Fu Yuehua, a woman arrested in Beijing on 18 January 1979 in connection with peasant demonstrations, was charged only two and a half months after her arrest. Throughout that period her relatives were not told where or why she was being detained; furthermore, they were still being denied permission to visit her at the time of her trial, nearly a year after her arrest. Xu Wenli, the editor of an unofficial journal, was arrested in connection with his publishing activities on 10 April 1981 but charged only four months later on 10 August 1981. Liu Qing, another editor, was held in detention in Beijing for nearly nine months without being charged or told the precise reason for his detention; his family was denied permission to see him throughout that period. Wang Xizhe and He Qiu, two workers from Guangzhou, were denied visits from relatives for over a year after their arrest and their families were not notified in advance of their trial.

In most of these cases, and in others, the prisoners are reported to have been tried in closed session without any advance notification given to their family. Despite that, it was officially claimed in some cases that they were given a "public" trial, apparently because a selected audience (which did not include their families) had been invited to attend. In Fu Yuehua's case, for instance, her family learned of her conviction from the newspapers the day after her trial. He Qiu's wife is said to have learned that her husband's trial was taking place while she was at work, and was therefore unable to attend it. The father of another prisoner of conscience, Liu Shanqing, was also informed about his son's trial after it had taken place despite having made repeated inquiries about his son's case for more than a year. Other examples have come to Amnesty

International's attention during the past year.

Categories

People who have been arrested in China in the past few years because of their opinions, beliefs or related non-violent activities can be divided into six broad categories, which overlap to a certain extent. They are:

1. Young workers and students who took part in a "democracy and human rights" movement which started in late 1978.

The arrest of a prisoner of conscience at the "democracy wall". Ren Wanding is arrested for putting up a poster criticizing the authorities' March 1979 ban on wall-posters considered "opposed to socialism". He was imprisoned apparently without trial from April 1979 to April 1981.

In October 1978 the Chinese authorities announced their decision to "rehabilitate" as "revolutionaries" people who, in April 1976, had demonstrated in Tian An Men Square in Beijing in support of the late Zhou Enlai's policies. Under the influence of radical leaders later stigmatized as the "Gang of Four", the demonstrations were declared a "counter-revolutionary" event and large numbers of people were arrested. In October 1976, however, the "Gang of Four" were arrested. The spontaneous demands for more freedom and democracy which had started during the Tian An Men demonstrations continued over the next two years. In Beijing wall-posters written by individuals were displayed at a major cross-road on a wall which was later known as the "democracy wall". Gradually, in 1978, the wall became a platform for calls for democratic reforms and human rights. The official "rehabilitation" of the 1976 demonstrators in the second half of 1978 gave further encouragement to what was already referred to as a "free-speech" or "democracy movement". In the main Chinese cities more and more wall-posters appeared. Young people gathered spontaneously in small groups and started publishing unofficial journals on political and literary matters. In Beijing, the journals included *Exploration*, the *April Fifth Tribune*, *Beijing Spring* and *Today*. Most of these journals emphasized the need to respect human rights and to stimulate free debate in Chinese society.

In March 1979, however, the authorities placed a ban on all wall-posters and publications which were considered to be "opposed to socialism and to the leadership of the Chinese Communist party",

Beijing municipal employees clean the "democracy wall" of wall-posters, December 1979.

and issued warnings to some young people whom they said were "going too far". Following this, several activists of the "democracy movement" were arrested. Despite the ban and the arrests, some of the unofficial journals continued publication for a while. Some contributors to the journals also organized study groups and circulated newsletters which—unlike the journals—were not sold publicly. They also raised questions about and circulated appeals on behalf of those arrested in 1979. As unofficial publishing had not been stopped completely, the authorities issued new warnings in mid-1980 stating that every publication had to be backed by a recognized organization responsible for it. In response to these new warnings, 29 unofficial

Artists and supporters of the "democracy movement" call for artistic freedom and democracy on a demonstration through the streets of Beijing, 1 October 1979. Prisoner of conscience Xu Wenli is second from the left. The banner reads: "demonstration for respect for the Constitution".

organizations formed the "National Association of Democratic Journals" in Guangzhou in October 1980, with its own publication *Zeren*, (Responsibility). However, in early 1981 the central authorities reportedly issued a directive to the local authorities asking them to ban all "illegal publications and organizations" and to investigate all people believed to have been connected with such organizations. The 20 main editors of unofficial journals were then arrested in April 1981 and others were arrested later in the year.

Most of the "democracy movement" activists who are now in prison were workers in their early thirties who had been students when the Cultural Revolution started (1966). Some had been imprisoned before for expressing their opinions. A few are reported to have been tried secretly in 1982 and sentenced to terms ranging from 10 to 15 years' imprisonment on "counter-revolutionary" charges. It is believed that others may have been convicted in closed trials at that time.

2. People detained apparently because they protested against human rights violations, including arbitrary arrests, or petitioned the authorities about their own grievances.

A number of people in this category are known to have been arrested in 1979 while the "democracy movement" and unofficial publishing were still tolerated. They included people known in China as "petitioners". By the end of 1978, hundreds of these had come to Beijing from various places in China—particularly from rural areas. Many were poor peasants who had come to present their grievances to the "central authorities" or to seek redress for miscarriages of justice. Others were unemployed people who claimed to have been the victims of injustice. The most outspoken petitioners, who organized public protests or demonstrations, are reported to have been arrested in early 1979 (such as Fu Yuehua, see page 21). The majority were reported at the time to have been either sent back to their original areas or to state farms near the capital. According to unofficial sources, some may also have been sent to "re-education-through-labour" farms or camps. People arrested in this category are usually sentenced to short-term imprisonment or assigned to carry out "re-education through labour" for up to three or four years.

3. Roman Catholic priests.

Several prisoners of conscience adopted by Amnesty International are elderly Roman Catholic priests who were arrested for the first time in the late 1950s. Soon after the establishment of the People's Republic of China in 1949, the government invited church leaders to a conference in Beijing, asking them to purge their churches of "foreign imperialist" influences and to cooperate with the government. Over the following years the authorities took steps to control religious affairs in China and strong pressure was put on the Chinese churches to sever their links with churches abroad. Such steps included the creation of the Chinese Patriotic Catholic Association, independent of the Vatican. Priests and bishops were pressed to join the association which soon started supervising the ordination of priests and other church affairs. Under pressure, the official Chinese Catholic Church severed its links with the Vatican and ceased to recognize the authority of the Pope. Some priests, however, opposed these changes and remained loyal to the Vatican. Many of them were arrested in 1955 during a campaign aimed at "weeding out counter-revolutionaries" from the administration, religious and industrial circles. They subsequently spent more than 20 years in prisons and labour camps. Some were arrested for the second time in 1981 after a brief period of freedom for persisting in their refusal to cooperate with the Patriotic Catholic Association and for carrying out religious activities independently from the official Church. Several of the priests are reported to have been brought to trial in 1983 and sentenced again to long prison terms in spite of being in their sixties, seventies or even eighties.

Shanghai Municipal Prison (rough map drawn by a former prisoner).

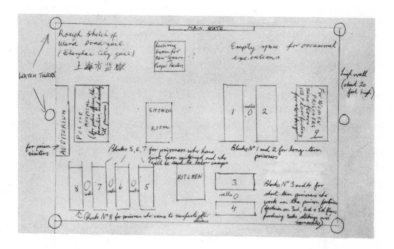

4. Tibetan nationals detained on religious grounds or accused of supporting regional independence.

Prisoners in this category include people arrested at various times for showing loyalty to the exiled spiritual leader of Tibetan Buddhists, the Dalai Lama, and other peaceful religious activities. At the time of the Cultural Revolution, people were reported to have been arrested merely for possessing photographs of the Dalai Lama or religious scriptures and paintings. Some people arrested on such grounds were reported to be still detained or restricted in the late 1970s. Recently, foreign journalists have reported that the policy towards religion of the Chinese authorities in Tibet is more relaxed. Most of the arrests reported to Amnesty International in recent years have appeared to be of people detained on political grounds, although religious feelings in Tibet are often connected with aspirations to independence; those who advocate the return of

16

the Dalai Lama to Tibet see him as both a religious and political leader. Some of the recent arrests were of people accused of shouting slogans in favour of the independence of Tibet. Others were suspected of connections with underground groups advocating independence. Among a number of people reported to have been arrested for political reasons in August 1983 in Lhasa was a young monk, Kalsang Tsering, aged 20. He is said to have been arrested on 26 August 1983, after talking to foreign journalists, for refusing to report on his interview to members of the Public Security Bureau.

Sangyip Prison in Lhasa (rough map drawn by a former prisoner).

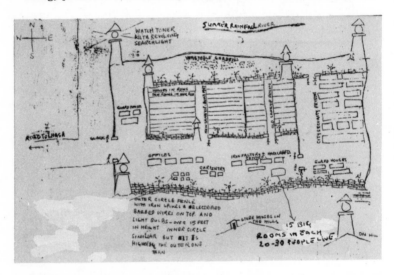

5. People accused of divulging "state secrets", "collecting intelligence" information, or passing on "secret" information to foreigners.

Although there is no strict definition of what constitutes a "state secret" in China, this term appears to be given a much broader meaning than in many other countries. It may cover, for instance, information published in magazines which, although not on sale to the general public, are available to many specialists or political cadres; it may also refer to party documents which despite not being publicly available have a very wide circulation. Amnesty International knows of several cases in which people were convicted of "collecting" or "divulging" or passing on to others information which would not have been considered secret in many other countries. Some have been officials. It is concerned that in some cases they have in fact been detained for exercising basic human rights, such as expressing opinions critical of aspects of Chinese society.

6. Officials reportedly arrested because of their political opinions or activities since the Cultural Revolution, who have been officially stigmatized as "leftists" during a campaign of "rectification" within the Chinese Communist Party which started in mid-1983.

Little information is available about such cases but some reports in the Chinese official press indicate that a few former officials may have been arrested for non-violent political offences since the start of this campaign. Yan Heitou, a former official from Wu'an district in Hebei province, was reported to have been rearrested shortly after his release from prison for making contact with his former "leftist comrades". According to the *Hebei Daily*, Yan Heitou was sent to prison in 1976 for taking part in the attempt by the "Gang of Four" to seize power and subsequently spent seven years in prison. His release sparked celebrations, the *Hebei Daily* said, and within a month dozens of his former comrades had come to him and expressed their disenchantment with the current situation. He was rearrested in late November 1983 (*Agence France Presse*, Beijing, 18 December 1983). Xu Guancheng, a former official in the Shanghai branch of the China Machinery Import and Export Corporation, was reported to have been arrested for organizing sit-in protests against his expulsion in 1982 from the Chinese Communist Party. Shanghai radio was reported to have said on 2 October 1983 that Xu Guancheng had been arrested following the discovery of a diary in which he had written "reactionary words and sentences to vent his dissatisfaction with the party organization and to attempt to reverse the verdict and stage a comeback".

Conditions of detention

Among the prisoners of conscience known to Amnesty International, several are alleged to have been subjected to some form of ill-treatment, usually during the first few months of their detention. In one case, that of Wei Jingsheng, solitary confinement for over four years is reported to have damaged the mental health of the prisoner. In most cases, although the information which led to the arrest may be well-documented, little is known about the prisoner once he or she has been detained and it is difficult to obtain information about the way in which individual prisoners of conscience are treated. Over the years, however, information provided by former prisoners held in various places across the country has tended to indicate some consistent patterns in the treatment of prisoners.*

Apart from complaints about their arbitrary detention and other aspects of the judicial system, former prisoners most often complain about the system of punishment and the inadequacy of food in detention. There appears to be a wide variation in general conditions of detention and in the type and quantity of food received by prisoners. Conditions vary in different areas and from one camp or prison to another. In some establishments conditions are described as generally adequate, but prisoners in some places appear to receive insufficient food with practically no proteins or vitamins. They are consequently reported to suffer malnutrition after relatively short periods in detention.

Although the ill-treatment of prisoners is prohibited by Chinese law, prisoners have been subjected to punishments which constitute ill-treatment according to international standards. Officials have acknowledged that there is a system of punishments—including solitary confinement—for prisoners who break prison rules. Prisoners are sometimes punished harshly just because they are considered "resistant" or because they complain about their treatment, according to former prisoners. This is particularly frequent during detention before trial when prisoners are held in isolation, usually for several months, and repeatedly interrogated, without being allowed to see their family, friends or a legal representative. Amnesty International believes that some of these punishments constitute cruel, inhuman and degrading treatment. They include the use of solitary confinement over prolonged periods**; the use of hand shackles—sometimes with the hands tied behind the back—day and night for days or weeks***; and other punishments such as beatings or being made to stand without moving for 24 hours without food. Such punishments are also used against convicted prisoners held in prisons or labour camps, although apparently more rarely than in detention centres.

Two former prisoners who to the best of Amnesty International's knowledge did not know each other and were held until recently in two different labour camps mentioned a punishment cell known as "xiaohao" (literally "small number") in their camps. This was a cell too small for anyone to stand up in. One prisoner reported that punishment in this cell could last from a few days to six months and that prisoners who had spent more than a few days in it had trouble

* This does not apply to the period of the Cultural Revolution when prisoners were frequently ill-treated and conditions of detention were generally harsher than at any other time since 1949.

** See the case of Wei Jingsheng.

*** See the case of Liu Qing.

walking when they were allowed out. Another prisoner stated that a healthy prisoner held in this cell for three months would suffer atrophy of the muscles. This punishment was reportedly used against prisoners who repeatedly "resisted" discipline.

Prisoners' profiles

The following pages illustrate the cases of people believed to be detained for exercising non-violently their fundamental human rights. Most of them have been adopted as prisoners of conscience by Amnesty International. Often, little information is available about such people and it is generally difficult to obtain information about prisoners after their arrest due to the isolation in which they are held, sometimes for long periods, to the secrecy surrounding political trials, and to the lack of response from the authorities to Amnesty International's inquiries.

The cases described in the following pages are those of people who have been arrested in the past five years (except for that of Bishop Gong). In some cases they had been arrested on a previous occasion. They are presented according to the date of arrest.

Gong Pinmei

Ignatius Gong Pinmei, the 84-year-old Roman Catholic Bishop of Shanghai, has spent nearly 30 years in prison since his arrest on 8 September 1955. He was sentenced to life imprisonment in 1960 on charges of leading a "counter-revolutionary clique under the cloak of religion". He is reported to be still detained in Shanghai's main prison.

Bishop Gong's arrest in 1955 took place during a national campaign against "counter-revolutionaries" aimed at people considered to be opposed to the Chinese Communist Party within the administration and in cultural, industrial and religious circles. Many Catholics and members of other religious groups were arrested at that time, in particular those who advocated that the churches should remain independent of interference by the government.

Bishop Gong's uncompromising stand on the independence of the Church from the government was known before his arrest. He is said to have refused to allow young members of his church to join communist groups and to have denied the sacraments to so-called "patriotic Catholics", members of the Chinese Patriotic Catholic Association established by the government in the mid-1950s to make the Roman Catholic Church in China independent of the Vatican. At the time of his arrest, he was accused of having formed with others a "counter-revolutionary clique" which had colluded "with the imperialists against the motherland under the cloak of religion". The charges against him and his "clique" included sabotaging the Catholic Patriotic movement; circulating rumours and advocating war; colluding with and offering shelter to imperialist spies; collecting restricted information; and trying to undermine the land-reform movement. It is believed, however, that the real reason for his arrest was his opposition to the government's interference in religious affairs.

After nearly five years in detention Bishop Gong was brought to trial in Shanghai. On 17 March 1960 he was sentenced to life imprisonment. Thirteen other priests—eight of them Jesuits—were tried at the same time and given terms ranging from five to 20 years' imprisonment. The trial was held *in camera* and no record of it is known to have been published apart from a press account by the official New China News Agency.

Bishop Gong reportedly spent several years in solitary confinement after his arrest and was prevented from seeing his family for many years.

A former prisoner, Dr Yi Lifa, who was imprisoned from 1963 to 1979, reportedly met Bishop Gong Pinmei at the time of the Cultural Revolution (1966-1968), in a labour camp in Anhui province. Dr Yi was then contemplating suicide and said that it was Bishop Gong who had dissuaded him. "Bishop Gong kept on praying, morning and evening, while he was working taking out the water buffaloes." After some prisoners reported this to the camp officials, a criticism meeting was organized and the other prisoners were encouraged to denounce Bishop Gong. "He stood calmly, his head down showing no emotion while I had to insult him," said Dr Yi. "I said 'if there is a God in heaven you would not be here'. He raised his head and looked at me strangely and I felt so bad." Several days later, Dr Yi was able to talk to Bishop Gong in the fields. The latter said he forgave him and encouraged him not to give up his struggle for life.*

According to more recent reports, Gong Pinmei has been held in Shanghai main prison for the last few years. He is reportedly held in relatively privileged conditions, being allowed to walk around

* Article by Henry Kamm in the *New York Times* of 25 May 1981, and Fox Butterfield, *China Alive in the Bitter Sea*, 1982, p. 368.

within the prison and to do traditional Chinese gymnastics. It has also been reported that the authorities would release him if he admitted that the government was justified in detaining him but that he has so far refused to do so.

Fu Yuehua

Fu Yuehua, a 37-year-old unemployed woman, was arrested in Beijing on 18 January 1979 for helping to organize a peasant demonstration. She was sentenced to two years' imprisonment a few months later. Some time after her release in 1981, she was reported to have been sent to a labour camp in the Beijing area. It is believed that she is still being denied her freedom.

Fu Yuehua was born in Beijing in 1947 in a workers' family. After the Cultural Revolution, she worked for Beijing Municipality and in 1971 was assigned a job as a construction worker in the Xuanwu district of the capital. Fu Yuehua was married to a graduate of Beijing University who had been sent to work in Hebei province and lived away from home. A wall-poster put up in late 1979 by a member of her family stated that soon after she started working in the Xuanwu district the Party Secretary of her work unit, Geng Yutian, made advances to her which she rebuffed. A few months later, the poster said, he accused her of being a "counter-revolutionary" during a political campaign. He then raped her on several occasions over a period of weeks. Fu suffered a nervous breakdown as a result, her family said, and had to go to hospital to be treated for schizophrenia; the construction company refused to pay her medical bills which amounted to about two years' salary. She was later unable to get her job back, to be transferred elsewhere or to find another job, her family stated, and her husband divorced her after being told by the construction company that it was she who had seduced the Party Secretary.

Fu Yuehua petitioned the authorities about her case for several years after this but without success. While petitioning the authorities about her own case, Fu Yuehua came to know many other petitioners who had suffered injustice. In late 1978 many came to Beijing from rural areas. She took a personal interest in their cases and, with her own experience of the administration in Beijing, helped them to present their demands. As many of the rural petitioners were illiterate, she also helped them to write wall-posters. On 8 January 1979, she participated in a demonstration of poor peasants in the streets of Beijing. She is said to have been among the demonstrators—many of them in rags—who were carrying banners calling for an end to "hunger and persecution" and demanding "democracy and human rights". She is also reported to have participated in another peasant demonstration on 14 January 1979.

Her arrest was first reported in wall-posters in Beijing around 24 January 1979. According to various sources she was arrested at home by the local police of her district early in the morning of 18 January 1979 and was subsequently held at the Gongdelin Detention Centre in Beijing. New wall-posters were put up in Beijing in February 1979 to protest against her arrest. They demanded that the authorities explain why she was being detained. According to a wall-poster signed by her family, by April 1979 her relatives had still not been told the reasons for her detention.

Official sources later revealed that she had been charged only on 3 April 1979—two and a half months after her arrest. In March 1979 the unofficial journal *Exploration (Tansuo)* published the testimony of a man who had been detained until mid-February 1979 in the Gongdelin Detention Centre. He alleged that Fu Yuehua had been ill-treated in detention, that she had been badly beaten by the police to make her "confess" and forced to take food when she went on hunger-strike to protest against her detention. There have been no official statements on these allegations and no explanation of the length of time she was held in detention without charge.

On 31 August 1979 Fu Yuehua was tried for the first time by Beijing Intermediate People's Court and sentenced to one year's imprisonment for "disrupting public order". She then appealed to Beijing High People's Court which, according to reports, found that the facts were "not clear" and the "evidence incomplete", and ordered a retrial.

She was brought to trial again on 17 October, but this time with one more charge: libel. Reporting her trial, the New China News Agency said that the charge of libel referred to Fu Yuehua's "continuing allegation" that she had been raped in 1972 by the Party Secretary of her work unit. The prosecution told the court that investigation had found the allegation to be "entirely false". However, at the end of one day the trial was adjourned when Fu Yuehua raised "certain new questions" which the court decided to investigate further "in accordance with the principle of not wronging the innocent" (New China News Agency, 17 October 1979). According to unofficial Chinese sources, Fu Yuehua had revealed details of

Geng Yutian's anatomy and had described the attack, and the selected audience, which included a number of jurists from outside Beijing, openly sympathized with her.

Her trial resumed on 24 December 1979 but no details of this hearing have emerged apart from an official report. According to this, Fu Yuehua was sentenced to two years' imprisonment on the charge of "disrupting public order". The charge of libel was dropped because, in the words of the court judge, "her libellous statements had not caused undue damage". The judge dismissed her charge of rape against Geng Yutian and said that she "was morally degenerate and had knowingly committed libel" (New China News Agency, 24 December 1979).

A few days after her trial it was reported that her family was still being denied permission to see her. According to unofficial sources, her brother went to Beijing Intermediate People's Court after learning of her conviction from the newspapers on 25 December, but was told that he could not see her.

Fu Yuehua was later reported to be held at Beijing Prison No. 1, the main prison in the capital. A prison spokesperson, Ren Licheng, stated on 13 May 1981 that she had been released from the prison in February that year after serving her sentence, but her whereabouts were not disclosed.

It was reported several months later that she had been sent to a labour camp at Liang Xiang, some 19 miles from Beijing, to keep her away from the capital. As far as is known, there had been no further legal proceedings against her. This camp holds mainly people assigned to "re-education through labour" without charge or trial. Fu Yuehua was held there until mid-1983 but it was reported that she "disappeared" from the camp around that time. There were rumours that she had been executed, but these have not been substantiated. She is believed to have been sent to a place of exile or detention in a remote province.

Wei Jingsheng

Wei Jingsheng, editor of one of the unofficial magazines banned in 1979, was tried in Beijing on 16 October 1979 for "counter-revolutionary crimes" and sentenced to 15 years' imprisonment and an additional three years' deprivation of political rights.

Wei Jingsheng, a 29-year-old electrician and editor of *Exploration*, was arrested at the end of March 1979, two days after Beijing Municipality declared a ban on all wall-posters and publications "opposed to socialism and to the leadership of the Chinese Communist Party".

An unofficial movement calling for "democracy and human rights" had developed in late 1978 after a relaxation in official policy had encouraged people to express their opinions and grievances. Wall-posters calling for democratic reforms and respect for human rights soon appeared in the main cities of China. Small unofficial magazines were started which often printed the texts of the wall-posters.

Between late 1978 and his arrest, Wei Jingsheng had published wall-posters and articles criticizing the political system in China and advocating democracy. In December 1978 he published an essay entitled "The Fifth Modernisation" in which he argued that China needed not only to modernize its economy but also a political modernization: democracy.

Wei Jingsheng was tried by Beijing Intermediate People's Court in October 1979 and convicted of passing on "military secrets" to a foreigner and conducting "counter-revolutionary propaganda and agitation" through his writings. The first charge refers to information about the Sino-Vietnamese conflict of March 1979. Wei Jingsheng was accused of having given it to a foreigner while the fighting was still going on. According to unofficial sources, this information had in fact been published in *Reference News*, an official paper circulated to a large number of cadres in China although not available to the general public.

The trial was not open to the public or to foreign observers although a selected audience—400 people according to official sources—was admitted into the courtroom. Those allowed in were given admission tickets in advance. Friends of Wei Jingsheng and others waiting outside the courtroom were refused entry.

Short extracts of the trial were shown on Chinese television. However, the official press did not publish any substantial report of the proceedings—only a summary of the prosecution case against Wei Jingsheng. The account of the trial published by the New China News Agency on 16 October 1979 did not mention any of the arguments put forward by Wei Jingsheng in his defence. This account revealed that the trial lasted just over seven hours and that the verdict was announced as follows:

> "In order to consolidate the dictatorship of the proletariat, safeguard the socialist system, ensure the smooth progress of socialist modernization and punish counter-revolutionary criminals, the chief judge said, the court had sentenced Wei Jingsheng to 15 years' imprisonment, depriving him of political rights for an additional three years in accordance with the provisions of article 2, item 1, under article 6, items 2 and 3, under article 10, article 16 and article 17 of the Act for the Punishment of Counter-revolution."
>
> (New China News Agency, 16 October 1979)

Shortly after the trial, an unofficial transcript of the proceedings was circulated in Beijing. It was distributed at the "democracy wall" by supporters of various unofficial magazines, some of whom were arrested after a large crowd had gathered to buy copies. The unofficial transcript was later published in Hong Kong and elsewhere. This was the first transcript of a Chinese dissenter's trial to become available outside China.

According to the unofficial transcript, three judges (one presiding judge and two assessors) conducted all the proceedings at the trial. This included the cross-examination of the defendant, Wei Jingsheng, and of the two prosecution witnesses. No defence witnesses were called in court. There was no defence lawyer, apparently because Wei Jingsheng had asked to conduct his own defence. The procurator read the charges against Wei Jingsheng at the beginning of the trial. The judge cross-examined the defendant and witnesses and the procurator then presented the indictment. Wei Jingsheng then read his defence statement and the procurator replied with a lengthy counter-argument. After an adjournment for a meeting of the "judicial committee", the Chief Judge announced the verdict.

Several aspects of the trial proceedings are particularly interesting. For instance, the judge who cross-examined Wei Jingsheng on the first charge—"passing on military secrets to a foreigner"—was mainly concerned with whether Wei Jingsheng knew he was doing something wrong when he gave information to a foreigner about China's conflict with Viet Nam. The question of whether or not this information was secret was not even mentioned in court, except by Wei Jingsheng. He said in his own defence that he never thought such information was secret as it was already circulating widely among Chinese citizens. The second charge—"conducting counter-revolutionary agitation and propaganda"—was based only on articles written by Wei Jingsheng criticizing China's leadership and social system. One such article, entitled "Democracy or a New Dictatorship", is attached in Appendix A. Extracts of this and other articles were cited in court as incriminating evidence.

The two witnesses brought to court by the prosecution had formerly been involved with *Exploration*, the unofficial magazine edited by Wei Jingsheng. They confirmed that Wei was the author of articles cited by the prosecution and gave information on his past activities and contacts with foreigners. One of the two witnesses, Yang Guang, mentioned in his testimony that on 4 February 1979 he had borrowed a report by Amnesty International from a foreign journalist. It concerned political prisoners in China and extracts were later printed in issues two and three of *Exploration*.

After the trial, Wei Jingsheng appealed against the verdict and the case was heard by the Beijing High People's Court on 6 November 1979. According to an official account, Wei Jingsheng had asked a member of the Beijing Lawyers Association to act as his defence lawyer in this new hearing. The High Court confirmed the verdict and sentence against him. Chinese law allows only one appeal against a verdict and the judgment of the High Court was final.

During the weeks after the trial the official Chinese press published many articles about Wei Jingsheng. They appeared to be running a campaign aimed at justifying the sentence against him and denigrating his character, as well as acting as a warning to other young activists.

During this press campaign, several unofficial publications in Beijing published articles and wall-posters in defence of Wei Jingsheng. They pointed out that even if Wei could be considered to have made a mistake by revealing information on the military situation, this could not be treated as "the crime of offering secret military intelligence to a foreigner". They also said that Wei had taken no action that constituted an "attempt to overthrow the dictatorship of the proletariat" and that, if no violence had been incited, it could not be said that a criminal act has occurred.

The large number of articles published in the official press justifying the verdict against Wei Jingsheng gives an indication of the significance of his case. As well as a warning to other activists, his trial marked the end of the period of liberalization which had started in 1978. During this period criticism of official policies, and unofficial publications, had been tolerated to a certain extent. According to unofficial Chinese sources, his trial was also meant to test reactions to the new laws and procedures due to come into force in January 1980.

Following his trial, Wei Jingsheng was reported to have been held for several years in solitary confinement in the detention centre adjacent to Beijing Prison No. 1. According to a former prisoner who was held in the Banbuqiao detention centre adjacent to the prison during 1980 and 1981, Wei Jingsheng was then detained in isolation in cell No. 11 of section 2—a block reserved for "major criminals". He reported that Wei Jingsheng went on hunger-strike once during that period, and that in April 1981 he was suddenly moved from his cell because he was constantly "making trouble" and it was feared that his rebellious spirit would influence the other prisoners.

In mid-1983 Wei Jingsheng was reported to be still confined in isolation in his cell, being allowed out for exercise only once a month and not allowed to meet other prisoners or to receive visits from his family. Amnesty International launched several appeals for his release and said it feared his health might be affected by the length of time he had spent in solitary confinement. The authorities, however, did not respond to these appeals. In May 1984 it was reported that Wei Jingsheng had twice been transferred to a hospital as his mental health had suffered, and he was reported to need treatment for schizophrenia. It was also rumoured that he had been transferred to a camp in Qinghai province, but this has remained unconfirmed. No further details of his health or whereabouts were available at the time of writing.

Liu Qing

Liu Qing, aged 37, former co-editor of an unofficial magazine, has been detained since 11 November 1979, when he was arrested in Beijing for selling the transcript of the trial of Wei Jingsheng. He was first sent to a labour camp and is reported to have been brought to trial in August 1982 in Beijing and sentenced to seven years' imprisonment.

A student at Nanjing University between 1973 and 1977, Liu Qing was subsequently sent to work as a machinist in a factory in the Nanjing area. He later moved to Beijing and was living there in late 1978 when the unofficial "democracy movement" started in the capital.

Liu Qing was one of the founders of the unofficial journal *April Fifth Tribune (Siwu Luntan)*. The first issue, on 16 December 1978, set out its main objective. This was to seek respect for the democratic freedoms guaranteed in the then constitution of the People's Republic of China, including freedom of expression and publication, and to "found a true socialist democracy" in the country.

During the following months, supporters of the *April Fifth Tribune* took part in meetings and demonstrations to protest against the arrests of several people involved in the "democracy movement" and other restrictions of fundamental freedoms. Among those arrested in Beijing in late March and early April 1979 were Wei Jingsheng, editor of the unofficial journal *Exploration*, and Ren Wanding, a founder of the "Chinese Human Rights Alliance". These arrests followed a ban imposed by the authorities in March 1979 on all wall-posters and publications considered to be "opposed to socialism and to the leadership of the Chinese Communist Party".

When the news of Wei Jingsheng's forthcoming trial emerged in mid-October 1979, Liu Qing tried to obtain official "admission tickets" to the trial. However, all the tickets had already been selectively distributed by the authorities. He later managed, nevertheless, to obtain recorded tapes of the trial. These he transcribed with the help of a few friends and on 9 November, they posted a notice on the "democracy wall" announcing that they would sell the transcript of Wei Jingsheng's trial two days later.

A large crowd of people gathered at the "democracy wall" on 11 November to buy the transcript. The police soon stepped in to stop the sale and arrested four of those selling the transcript. Liu Qing escaped arrest due to the confusion which followed the police intervention. However, when he went that evening with several friends to Beijing Police Headquarters to inquire about those arrested he was himself detained. Most of those arrested on 11 November 1979 are reported to have been subsequently released, but Liu Qing has remained in detention ever since.

A 196-page testimony by Liu Qing describing his arrest and detention was published outside China in late 1981. It was the text of a long letter dated January 1981 which Liu Qing had addressed to the Chinese authorities from the camp where he was being held. It was handwritten and has been authenticated by friends of Liu Qing as being in his handwriting. According to the testimony, Liu Qing spent several months in the detention centre of Beijing Prison No. 1 after his arrest in November 1979. For the first five months he was held in solitary confinement in a cold and wet cell. He developed rheumatism in his left side and difficulty in walking, his hair began to fall out and his eyesight deteriorated. For some of that period his cell was lit 24 hours a day; sometimes it was painfully bright and at other times too dim to read.

In April 1980 Liu Qing was moved from solitary confinement to a large shared cell. When he was taken out for exercise, he refused to clasp his hands below his stomach as the warders required since he considered it demeaning. He was beaten and rushed back to his cell. He wrote:

> "When I was brought back to the cell my body was covered with blue and purple bruises from the beating. I had been forced to wear a gas mask that made it very hard for me to breathe, and I was restricted with handcuffs that cut into my flesh."

The testimony included accounts of other prisoners ill-treated in the detention centre where he was held.

Liu Qing said that throughout his detention in Beijing, his family was not able to visit him or exchange correspondence with him, nor were they informed of the reason for his arrest. According to his testimony he addressed two letters to the authorities to protest against his illegal detention and treatment in the detention centre. He reported giving the first letter on 21 January 1980 to a prison guard who promised to transmit it to Beijing People's Procuratorate and the second one to another guard on 5 April 1980. He received neither a reply nor an acknowledgement to either letter.

In mid-1980 Liu Qing was assigned to three years' "re-education through labour" in a labour camp. His family was then reportedly informed that this was based on three grounds: taking part in a demonstration by peasants in Beijing in January 1979; participating in the sale of the transcript of Wei Jingsheng's trial; and stealing and making out false sickness certificates (an allegation which his family rejected as unfounded). Liu Qing was sent to the "Temple of the Lotus Flower" labour camp in Shaanxi province. He was reportedly informed for the first time that he had been "assigned" to three years of "re-education through labour" only after his arrival there. At the camp, according to his account, both convicted prisoners and people undergoing "re-education through labour" were forced to do hard labour, transporting heavy stones; the camp was surrounded by high walls topped by electrified wire and guarded by armed soldiers and police dogs.

It was reported in late 1982 that Liu Qing had been transferred to Beijing and tried there secretly in August 1982. No official information has been made public about the trial and the specific charges brought against him are not known. He is said to have been sentenced to seven years' imprisonment for "counter-revolutionary" offences. These are believed to be connected to the publication abroad of his testimony. His brother, Liu Nianchun, and Lu Lin, an editor of *Exploration*, are also reported to have been brought to trial in Beijing at the same time and sentenced to 10 and four years' imprisonment respectively. Both are believed to have been tried and sentenced for being involved in the circulation of Liu Qing's testimony, but no details are known about their trial.

Support for Liu Qing's release was expressed publicly inside China itself. Eleven organizations associated with the "democracy movement" protested against his detention on 20 May 1980 in a leaflet distributed in Beijing. In October 1980 the representatives of some 16 unofficial journals from different provinces also formed a "National Committee to save Liu Qing".

Liu Qing is reported to be held at Beijing Prison No. 1.

Lobsang Chodag

Lobsang Chodag, a worker in a truck-repair shop in Lhasa, in the Autonomous Region of Tibet, has been detained since March or April 1980, when he was reportedly arrested for putting up wall-posters in the streets and accused of being a member of an underground Tibetan youth organization. He was last reported to have been held in Sangyip and Drapchi prisons in Lhasa.

Lobsang Chodag is reported to have been arrested some time after wall-posters advocating the independence of Tibet had appeared in Lhasa, probably to coincide with the anniversary of the Tibetan uprising of March 1959 against Chinese rule in Tibet. According to foreign journalists and other sources, Tibetans advocating the independence of Tibet distribute clandestine literature and put up posters on such occasions. Underground organizations of young dissidents reportedly meet in private homes and transmit information about the exiled Dalai Lama in India and about religion to their followers. It is also reported that they monitor Indian radio broadcasts for information from the exiled spiritual leader.

According to information received by Amnesty International, at the time of his arrest Lobsang Chodag's house was searched but no document showing involvement with an underground organization was found. He is said to have denied the accusations. It is also alleged that Lobsang Chodag was brutally treated after his arrest: that his jaw was broken and he could not eat for a time. Little information has become available about his condition since then.

Lobsang Chodag has never—to the best of Amnesty International's knowledge—been charged or tried. Nor has another Tibetan youth, Topgyal, reported to have been arrested at the same time, for similar reasons. Lobsang Chodag's mother, Tsering Lhamo, is said to have been herself arrested in April 1980 when she protested against her son's detention, and to have been imprisoned for about a year in Drapchi prison in Lhasa. She had been previously detained briefly in October 1979 for shouting slogans in favour of Tibetan independence during the visit to Lhasa of a delegation of Tibetan exiles.

In early 1984 Amnesty International received information indicating that Lobsang Chodag might be released. However, no confirmation had been received by June 1984.

Xu Wenli

Xu Wenli, former editor of an unofficial journal, was sentenced to 15 years' imprisonment on charges of "counter-revolutionary" activity, after being arrested in Beijing in April 1981.

Xu Wenli, the son of a doctor, was born in 1945 in Anqing City, Anhui province. He is married and has a daughter. On leaving school in 1963 he joined the army, and after being demobilized from the army became a maintenance electrician in Beijing. In 1979 Xu Wenli joined Liu Qing to found the unofficial journal *April Fifth Tribune*. This became the most widely circulated unofficial journal in North China. It continued to appear despite the arrest in November 1979 of Liu Qing, one of its chief editors. However, Xu Wenli and the group who ran the journal decided voluntarily to cease publication in early 1980 after strong warnings from the authorities to those who continued to publish unofficial journals despite the ban imposed in March 1979.

After publication of the journal had been suspended, Xu Wenli and his friends circulated a private newsletter, the *Study Bulletin*. Xu also edited two other journals, *Contemporary Matters* and

Humanity. The *April Fifth Tribune* was revived for a period in November 1980, but Xu Wenli was then succeeded by Yang Jing as its chief editor.

Xu Wenli was a vocal member of the "democracy movement" in Beijing and was interviewed on several occasions by foreign journalists. In these interviews in 1980, he stressed the need for reform and democracy under the leadership of the Communist Party. He told journalists that he considered himself a Marxist; he also insisted that "democratic socialism" could not be "achieved by police action". Xu denied the insinuation voiced at that time by Vice-Premier Deng Xiaoping that the "democracy movement" activists were anti-socialist. In March 1980 he was reported to have said:

"They say now that we are anti-communist and anti-socialist. But who in fact is anti-communist and anti-socialist? Is it us? I think it is a group within the Communist Party itself which is opposing the people in various ways.

"It is true that there are people within the Party who use power to oppress people. I am just a small electrician who fixes lights. I have no power, but some of these people suggest we are like devils preying on the people."

(*Reuters*, Beijing, 20 March 1980)

Xu Wenli is also reported to have appealed to the authorities on 10 January 1981 about Liu Qing's detention.

According to Chinese sources, Xu Wenli was taken from his home by the police at midnight on 10 April 1981. The police reportedly confiscated his tape recordings and personal papers. Yang Jing is reported to have been arrested on the same day.

Xu Wenli is reported to have been held in the detention centre of Beijing Prison No. 1 after his arrest and to be held there still. According to various sources, he was tried in Beijing on 8 June 1982 and sentenced to 15 years' imprisonment plus four years' deprivation of political rights for "organizing a counter-revolutionary group" and "counter-revolutionary propaganda and agitation".

In October 1982 a Hong Kong Chinese language review, *Baixing*, published a document which it said is the text of the court judgment against Xu Wenli, detailing the accusations against him.* It states that he was tried on 8 June 1982 by Beijing Intermediate People's Court in the presence of a judge and two people's assessors and that he was assigned a lawyer from the Legal Counsel Office of Beijing Municipality. It also states that Xu Wenli was formally charged only on 10 August 1981, four months after his arrest, and

---

* A full translation of this document is included in Appendix B.

that he was tried "in open court according to the law". A long list of goods confiscated from Xu Wenli's house was appended to the document. These included a printing machine, 19 volumes of notebooks and 21 reels of tape recordings, as well as a large number of Chinese language magazines from Hong Kong.

According to the document two main accusations were brought against Xu Wenli. First, that he organized a meeting in Beijing in June 1980 together with others who are named in the document in order to "plot" the setting up of a "counter-revolutionary organization". This, the document says, was to be a "new form of proletarian political party" to "destroy the dictatorship of one party". Preparations allegedly involved the publication of the *Study Bulletin* (mentioned above) and making contacts with people in Hong Kong and other places. Those named in the document as being part of this "plot" are Wang Xizhe (from Guangzhou), Sun Weibang (from Qingdao), Xu Shuiliang (from Nanjing), Fu Shenqi (from Shanghai) and Liu Er'an (from Anyang). The document also states that "others" were involved. Second, Xu Wenli was accused of "carrying out incitement through counter-revolutionary propaganda" through his speeches, articles, essays and leaflets. In particular, he was accused of denouncing "the strangulation of democracy" which resulted from the ban on posters and unofficial publications imposed in March 1979 by the authorities, and of having "opposed the legal authorities in their just decisions on counter-revolutionary elements". The accusations against Xu Wenli, according to this document, involved only the peaceful exercise of fundamental human rights.

To Amnesty International's knowledge the Chinese authorities have not made public any information about Xu Wenli's trial. Nor have they replied to several inquiries made by the organization about it.

Fu Shenqi

Fu Shenqi, a factory worker and editor of two unofficial journals, was arrested in Beijing in early April 1981 during the wave of arrests of supporters of the "democracy movement".

Fu Shenqi, aged 30, is from Shanghai, where he worked in a power plant from 1971. In the late 1970s he edited unofficial journals in his spare time. He was arrested in Beijing when he went there to discuss with the authorities the citizens' right to publish unofficial magazines. In October 1980 he became the chief editor of *Responsibility (Zeren)*, the journal of the National Association of Democratic Journals founded in October 1980 to represent unofficial publications throughout China.

Fu Shenqi was born in 1954 in a worker's family in Shanghai and studied at Shanghai's Jingyie Junior High School from 1968 to 1971. When he graduated he went to work in a Shanghai motor factory. In the same year he passed the entrance examination for Shanghai Normal College Number Four. However, the following year he became ill and asked to leave the college and return to his factory. At some time he became a member of the Chinese Communist Youth League.

In 1978 he became active in the "democracy movement" which developed at that time. He organized a reform group, the "Regeneration Society", which was later disbanded. In 1979 he cooperated with others to found the unofficial journal *Voice of Democracy (Minzhu Zhisheng)* in Shanghai. The authorities declared the journal to be "anti-Party and anti-socialist" when it came out in support of Polish workers "fighting for democracy and against bureaucratic tyranny".

In April 1980 members of the "democracy movement" stood in elections in several cities. Fu Shenqi stood as a candidate in the local elections for People's Representatives in a southern district of Shanghai. This was the first time since the early 1960s that there had been open competition in an election.

On 29 April 1980 Fu Shenqi distributed his first election campaign leaflet at his factory. In the leaflet he reportedly stated that he loved his motherland, accepted the "correct leadership of the Chinese Communist Party" and was prepared to sacrifice his "life and energy for the modernization of the political system". During the election campaign in May, he called meetings and circulated other leaflets to the workers of his factory. However, according to his own account of the election campaign which was later published in Hong Kong, the Party Leadership Committee in his factory held a series of meetings to criticize him, accusing him of being involved in "anti-Party and anti-socialist" activities. Although Fu Shenqi came second with 43 per cent of the vote in the first round of primary elections, he reportedly failed to be elected because of the opposition of the Party Leadership Committee in his factory.

Little has been heard of Fu Shenqi since his arrest. He is believed to have been brought to trial and sentenced as his name was reportedly mentioned during the trial of Xu Wenli. Fu Shenqi and others were accused of taking part in Xu Wenli's "counter-revolutionary" group. It was stated that they would be brought to trial separately. It has also been reported that Fu Shenqi was ill-treated in detention, but few details are available. According to reports Fu Shenqi was once taken from prison to his factory for a criticism meeting, but collapsed during the meeting. Amnesty International has not received any recent news of him despite repeated inquiries to the Chinese authorities about his case.

Wang Xizhe

On 20 April 1981 Wang Xizhe, a factory worker from Guangzhou (Canton City) and editor of an unofficial journal, was arrested for the third time since the Cultural Revolution. He was sentenced to 14 years' imprisonment in May 1982 for "counter-revolutionary" activities.

Wang Xizhe, aged 35, is well known in China as one of the authors of a wall-poster which was displayed in the streets of Guangzhou in November 1974. The poster was unusual in its contents and in its length—it covered about a hundred yards of wall and was entitled "Concerning Socialist Democracy and Legal System". It was signed Li Yizhe, a pseudonym formed from the names of its three authors: *Li* Zhengtian, Chen *Yi*yang and Wang Xi*zhe*. The poster immediately attracted enormous attention in Guangzhou and was photographed by travellers. Copies eventually reached Hong Kong where it was reprinted and circulated. It criticized Lin Biao, former Vice-Chairman of the Communist Party who reportedly disappeared in 1971 after an attempted "coup" and was criticized throughout China between 1972 and 1974. In theory, therefore, the criticism of Lin Biao in the Li Yizhe poster did not contradict the official policy of the time. However, the poster went beyond formal criticism of Lin Biao and raised issues relating to repression, democracy and the legal system in China.

The impact of the Li Yizhe poster appears to have been enormous. Its authors were at first criticized and placed "under surveillance". However, in March 1977 the "Li Yizhe" group was declared "counter-revolutionary" by Guangdong province Party Committee. Several hundred people were reportedly implicated. Li Zhengtian, Chen Yiyang and Wang Xizhe were then imprisoned. Their case was later reviewed along with many others following the fall of the "Gang of Four". They were released and rehabilitated in January 1979, just as a "democracy movement" was beginning in China.

Wang Xizhe had been imprisoned previously for a short period. Like many young students who participated in the Cultural Revolution, he had been arrested in 1968 and detained for a year. After his release, he had been exiled to work in the countryside in the north of Guangdong province, but his parents managed to have him returned to Guangzhou as he was an only son. Wang then found a job in a factory.

After his release from prison in January 1979, Wang Xizhe wrote a theoretical article entitled "Struggle for the class dictatorship of the proletariat" which was published in July 1979 in the Guangzhou unofficial journal *Voice of the People*. In this and subsequent articles he made his views known, criticizing a workers' state where the leadership "will become alienated into something opposed to the proletariat". He later became editor of the unofficial journal *Learners' Bulletin* in Guangzhou and an associate of the *April Fifth Tribune* published in Beijing by Xu Wenli, Liu Qing and others.

Some time after the arrest of Liu Qing in November 1979, a number of activists from all over China formed a "National Committee for the Release of Liu Qing". Wang Xizhe joined the committee. In an interview on 26 December 1980 he reported on the results of appeals for Liu Qing and Wei Jingsheng made by the "National Committee for the Release of Liu Qing":

"For a variety of reasons, its work has made little progress to date, but comrades in Peking, Shanghai and Wuhan are still striving hard to secure the release of Liu Qing. We have made representations to official departments but these have not met with any conspicuous success. Where we have had quite a degree of success, however, has been in the raising of the case of Wei Jingsheng by local election candidates in the West Ward of Peking. Wei Jingsheng's case is directly related to that of Liu Qing, and as a result of the matter having been raised, the Higher Court of Peking has subsequently brought forth the evidence upon which it had convicted Wei Jingsheng; after its publication, this material met with criticism and rebuttal from unofficial people's organizations through the country, including from the Guangdong journal *Responsibility*."

(New Left Review, No. 131)

In the same interview Wang Xizhe referred to the "National Association of Democratic Journals" founded in Guangzhou in October 1980 by some 29 unofficial organizations from all over China after the authorities warned that every publication required a recognized organization to accept responsibility for it. The association had its own journal *Responsibility (Zeren)*, of which Wang Xizhe was co-editor.

In 1980 Wang Xizhe reportedly wrote an "Open Letter to the National People's Congress Concerning the Arrest of Liu Qing". One of the charges brought against him at his trial was based on this open letter. In it he is said to have protested against the arbitrary nature of Liu Qing's detention and to have defended in the following terms the way in which Liu Qing had publicized Wei Jingsheng's trial:

> "Why is it that while direct knowledge of the proceedings was permitted, means of transmitting this knowledge by indirect means was not permitted? Why is it that the right to direct attendance of Wei's trial was protected by national law but the indirect reading about and verbal communication of the trial's proceeding was a crime punishable by law? Liu Qing and the *April Fifth Tribune*'s publicizing of the minutes of the Wei trial is in fact protected in the clauses of the Constitution; it is the Beijing Court's declaration of Liu's 'guilt' that has caused the 'crime'."
> (Human Rights Internet Reporter, 7.5, June—August 1982)

Wang Xizhe was arrested on 20 April 1981 at his factory and it is reported that the police seized some 350 documents and other items belonging to him. Despite repeated requests his family was refused permission to visit him in prison for over a year, according to sources in Hong Kong; his relatives were not notified in advance of his trial and were unable to attend it. However, according to a delegation of students from Hong Kong who went to Guangzhou to inquire about his trial, officials of Guangzhou Intermediate People's Court told them that Wang Xizhe had been granted a "public trial" attended by some 40 people. To Amnesty International's knowledge no official information was made public about the trial or the verdict.

Wang Xizhe is reported to have been tried on 28 May 1982 and sentenced to 14 years' imprisonment and four and a half years' deprivation of political rights under Articles 98 and 102 of the Criminal Law. He is said to have been charged with "inciting the masses to resist arrest and violate the law and statute of the state"; "counter-revolutionary propaganda and agitation"; and "actively taking part in a counter-revolutionary group". The first charge referred to Wang's open letter about Liu Qing which was quoted at the trial as evidence that he had incited violations of the law, according to reports. The second charge was reportedly based on the political views he expressed in his speeches and articles and the third charge on his close association with other activists of the "democracy movement", in particular with Xu Wenli. According to the unofficial text of the judgment on Xu Wenli, Wang Xizhe was accused of taking part in Xu Wenli's "counter-revolutionary" group and of participating in "secret meetings" in Beijing between 10 and 12 June 1980. These were allegedly aimed at the eventual creation of a "new form of proletarian political party" with the intention of "destroying the dictatorship of one party".

All information available on Wang Xizhe's trial indicates that he was accused only of activities involving the non-violent exercise of fundamental human rights. No news of him has been received by Amnesty International since his trial and his present whereabouts are unknown.

Tao Sen

Tao Sen, a student, has been detained since mid-1981 for taking a leading part in student protests against electoral irregularities at his college.

Tao Sen was born in Liuyang (Hunan province) in central China in 1948. He is said to be from a family of cadres who participated in the "Long March" in the 1930s and who joined the Chinese Communist Party in the early stages of the Chinese revolution. In 1966 he graduated from high school in Liuyang and joined the Communist Youth League in July that year. At the start of the Cultural Revolution in 1966, he is reported to have been a Red Guard leader in Changsha. He was later downgraded from "leader" to "security officer", reportedly because of his opposition to ill-treating teachers. He soon resigned and returned to Liuyang where he was a manual worker. At that time Tao Sen's father is reported to have been criticized for praising two disgraced former leaders, but he was rehabilitated by the central government in 1975.

In 1970 Tao Sen was transferred to work in a fertilizer factory and he was transferred again later for criticizing the Party Secretary of the factory and another factory official. In 1973 he was accepted by the Mathematics department of the University of Wuhan (the capital of Hubei province) but his entrance application was subsequently rejected, reportedly on the grounds that he "used his father's background". Tao Sen sent petitions to Beijing in 1975 and 1977 to protest against being refused entry at Wuhan University. In 1977 he was admitted at the Hunan Teachers' Training College in Changsha (the capital of Hunan province).

In 1980 elections were held in some parts of China for local people's congresses. Elections took place in some large work units such as factories, colleges and universities. Tao Sen stood as a candidate in the elections at the Hunan Teachers' Training College which were held in late September and October 1980.

The unofficial Shanghai journal *Voice of Democracy* (No. 6) and the Hong Kong magazine *The Seventies* (September 1981) reported that three rounds of primary elections were held at the college between 22 September and 6 October 1980 to nominate the candidates who would participate in the final election. However, the college administration then organized a fourth and fifth round of primary elections, apparently unhappy about the outcome of the first three. On 9 October college officials announced that there were *seven* official candidates (among them Tao Sen), although they had said on 8 October, after the fourth round of primary elections, that they would make public the names of *six* official candidates on the following day. These discrepancies and manipulations angered the students, who gathered to demand an explanation from the college administration. The Vice-President, Su Ming, then reportedly dismissed their demands rudely and refused to talk to them.

This triggered further discontent among the students. During the night of 9 October they organized a demonstration to petition the provincial authorities: 2,000 students reportedly took part. They elected a delegation of 21 people with Tao Sen as their general representative, to demand that an investigation into the elections be held and the results reconsidered. The provincial authorities, however, supported the college administration. The students then organized further demonstrations and a hunger-strike over the following days. By 15 October, their protest had gained the support of students in other universities and colleges in Changsha.

The protest was considered sufficiently serious for the central authorities to despatch officials from Beijing to deal with it. These held discussions with the student representatives on 20 October, but with no result. Tao Sen then called a meeting where it was decided that a "petition team" including 21 student representatives would be sent to Beijing to report directly to the central authorities. The team arrived in Beijing on 29 October, where they were received by representatives of the Party Central Committee and State Council. They returned to Hunan on 11 November 1980. It is reported that the central authorities had stated that the college administration had committed errors in handling the elections and that the Vice-President, Su Ming, should present a self-criticism for his rude attitude to the students. They also decided that the election held on 14 October should be proclaimed invalid and the election carried out again.

According to the Hong Kong magazine *The Seventies*, these conclusions and others were written down in *Document No. 60* of the Election Office of the National People's Congress (NPC), after an investigation team had concluded a two-week investigation at the college in November 1980. The document listed eight points including those mentioned above. The last point was a recommendation that there be no retaliation against students who had participated in petitions and sit-ins. This document, however, came from the government (rather than from the Party) and it is reported that although the college authorities did make public a written "self-examination", they refused later to accept the conclusions of the document on the grounds that this was not "the voice of the Party Central Committee".

There was a general hardening of official attitudes towards young dissenters and unofficial publications in early 1981. This resulted in the arrests of over 30 supporters of the "democracy movement" throughout China in April 1981 and the following months. At the Hunan Teachers' Training College the authorities reportedly began publicly criticizing Tao Sen and another candidate in the October 1980 elections, Liang Heng. When a wall-poster criticizing the college authorities was put up in the college this was described by officials as a "counter-revolutionary" incident, and an investigation was immediately launched. Tao Sen was eventually arrested, probably in May or early June 1981. On 19 June 1981, the college authorities announced that he had lost his student status and had been expelled from the college. A few hours later the Hunan provincial Public Security Bureau (police) assigned him to three years' "re-education through labour", an administrative punishment imposed without the accused being formally charged or tried.

According to information received by Amnesty International a news item posted on a blackboard at Nanjing University in early November 1981 revealed some information on the official grounds for his detention. This news item, reprinted from *The Students*

Union's Newsletter (Xuelian Tongxun), said (in approximate translation):

> "Tao Sen, the 1977 entry student of Hunan Teachers' Training College, has since September last year [i.e. 1980] been exploiting some existing shortcomings in the school's preparational work for the election of the District Representatives to criticize the Communist Party of China and the socialist system. He has spread malicious rumours. He has had contacts with illegal organizations and illegal publications, as well as with suspect visitors from abroad. His activities have had a spreading effect and have had serious results. Therefore, the college authorities have decided to expel Tao Sen from the College. The Hunan Public Security Bureau has given Tao Sen three years of re-education through labour."

Tao Sen is reported to have been sent to a labour camp in You county, Hunan province. He was due for release in mid-1984. However, no recent news of him has been received by Amnesty International.

Xu Shuiliang

Xu Shuiliang, a 31-year-old worker in a pharmaceutical factory in Nanjing, was arrested in July 1981 in connection with the arrests of other editors and supporters of unofficial journals throughout China. He had previously been imprisoned for three years for putting up wall-posters in the streets of Nanjing in 1975.

Xu Shuiliang is said to have been from a poor peasant family. He was a student at Zhejiang University when the Cultural Revolution started in 1966. Like many students at the time, he took an active part in the Cultural Revolution. He later went to work at Nanjing pharmaceutical factory and became a member of the workers' theoretical group in the factory. He stayed there until his first arrest in 1975.

According to an article in the Hong Kong review *Dong Xiang* of 16 February 1979, in mid-1975 Xu Shuiliang displayed publicly a series of posters criticizing the "bureaucratic elite" and the system of privileges in Chinese society. One of these was a 10-sheet long poster commenting on the political situation which he put up in the streets of Nanjing on 11 September 1975. According to this report, it was torn down the same evening by the municipal cleaning team, and the Jiangsu Party Committee sent a "theoreticians team" to the pharmaceutical factory where Xu Shuiliang worked to criticize him. The team organized a face-to-face debate with Xu Shuiliang, but was reportedly defeated in open argument. On 27 November 1975 the provincial Party Committee ordered the leadership of the pharmaceutical factory to organize a "big criticism meeting" against Xu in the factory. Xu answered some of the accusations during the meeting, but a member of the municipal Public Security Bureau announced that, "at the strong request of the masses", he was arresting the "anti-party, anti-socialist element" Xu Shuiliang.

Xu Shuiliang was then imprisoned. According to the report in *Dong Xiang*, after three months of investigation his case was still pending and no formal charges had been brought against him. His friends then heard that his detention had been extended indefinitely because he had committed "new crimes" while in detention. His case was still not resolved three years later and he was still in prison without having been charged in early 1979. He is reported to have been held at Wawa Qiao prison in Nanjing for the three years of his detention.

While there, he came to know other political detainees who, once released, protested publicly against his continued detention. It is reported in particular that they put up posters in the streets of Nanjing in January 1979 asking that he be rehabilitated. They compared him to a well-known group of dissidents who had written a long poster under the pseudonym Li Yizhe and had been imprisoned; their case had been reviewed after the fall of the "Gang of Four" and they were finally released and rehabilitated in January 1979.

Xu Shuiliang was released in 1979 but the precise date is not known; little information is available about his subsequent activities. It is reported that he wrote several articles for unofficial journals after his release. These included articles entitled "The transitional process from capitalism to socialism", "On the state and classes", "On unity and struggle" and "The problem of socialist distribution".

Xu Shuiliang is reported to have been arrested once more in July 1981, presumably in Nanjing. Little has been heard of him since. However, his name was mentioned in the court judgment against Xu Wenli (see p. 33). According to this document, Xu Shuiliang was accused with others from other cities of belonging to Xu Wenli's "counter-revolutionary group". The document said that they were all to be "dealt with separately". This indicates that Xu Shuiliang and the others involved have probably been brought to trial.

Dai Zhen

Dai Zhen, a 50-year-old official from Guangzhou (Canton City), was sentenced to 12 years' imprisonment in December 1982 on charges of "stealing state secrets and selling them". Amnesty International believes that he was arrested and tried for expressing views critical of government policies and has adopted him as a prisoner of conscience. Information about Dai Zhen's case has been published in two official newspapers from Guangzhou—the *Nanfang Daily (Nanfang Ribao)* and the *Yangcheng Evening News (Yangcheng Wanbao)*—and by the Hong Kong magazine implicated in the case, *Zheng Ming*.

According to information received by Amnesty International, Dai Zhen became the Deputy Director of the office of the United Front Work department in Guangzhou in 1981, having previously been a cadre in local government offices for many years. He had lived in Hong Kong between 1948 and 1950. He went there in 1948 to escape arrest by the Guomindang (Nationalist government). Before that he had been a student at Shanghai University and a leader of the student movement opposed to the Guomindang. While in Hong Kong he became a reporter for the paper *Wen Hui Bao*, and established contacts with journalists there.

From 1978 Dai Zhen wrote articles under a pseudonym for the Hong Kong magazine *Zheng Ming*. In these articles he criticized certain Chinese Government policies, and argued that democratic reforms were needed. He also wrote about political and social affairs in Guangzhou city. It is said that he generally mailed his articles directly to *Zheng Ming* but sometimes gave them to people travelling from Guangzhou to Hong Kong. *Zheng Ming* paid him HK$500 per month for his articles. This money was not always given to him in cash but sometimes in goods bought for him in Hong Kong at his request. It is said that whatever was bought for him was deducted from his wages. At the time of his trial the fact that he was receiving money and goods from Hong Kong was used by newspapers in Guangzhou to denigrate him (see below).

Dai Zhen is reported to have been arrested in August 1981. An article in the *Nanfang Daily* of 5 September 1981 stated:

> "The People's Procuratorate of Guangzhou city has recently approved the arrest of Dai Zhen, Deputy Director of the Party Office of the United Front Work of Guangzhou city, who has leaked important Party and State secrets. This case will be heard by the Political-Legal department.
>
> "In the course of his duty, Dai Zhen used the facilities provided by his position to transgress the State and Party

44

regulations on the protection of state secrets. From April till July this year, he secretly sent to a magazine in Hong Kong several articles divulging important state secrets and criticizing the Party and the State. Furthermore, he received bribes, including a refrigerator and other goods, as well as several thousand Hong Kong dollars.

"Dai Zhen has violated the law knowingly: the circumstances are serious; he has violated the Criminal Law, committing the crime of leaking state secrets; he must be investigated according to the law to determine his culpability."

(*Nanfang Daily*, 5 September 1981)

Dai Zhen was brought to trial in December 1982. The trial was not held publicly and no information is available about the procedures followed. However, the verdict was published in the *Yangcheng Evening News* and the *Nanfang Daily* on 23 December 1982. These two newspapers also published several articles denigrating Dai Zhen during December 1982, presumably during the trial itself. The following is a summary translation of an article in the *Nanfang Daily* reporting on the verdict:

"The former Deputy Director of the Party Office of the United Front Work of Guangzhou city, Dai Zhen, used his power and position for many years to steal important Party and State secrets and sell them to Wen Hui, the editor-in-chief of the Hong Kong magazine *Zheng Ming*, and other people. He thus received over HK$10,000 as well as some goods . . .

"Recently, Guangzhou High People's Court sentenced Dai Zhen to 12 years' imprisonment according to Article 97 of the Criminal Law of the PRC and confiscated all the property he had illegally obtained.

"In March 1978, not long after Dai Zhen became acquainted with Wen Hui (the editor-in-chief of the Hong Kong monthly *Zheng Ming*), he accepted Wen Hui's suggestion to contribute articles to *Zheng Ming*, supplied him with internal secrets and received goods from him.

"In May 1979, Wen Hui sent his wife to Guangzhou to find out whether Dai Zhen was satisfied with the goods supplied and propose from then on to remunerate him with HK$500 per month. Dai Zhen still requested a refrigerator and other goods (. . .). From then on, to comply with Wen Hui's wish, Dai Zhen used various means to obtain State

and Party secrets (. . .) and started taking a criminal path
. . .''

(*Nanfang Daily*, 23 December 1982)

The editors of the Hong Kong magazine *Zheng Ming* issued a public statement refuting the accusations after Dai Zhen's trial. In particular, it stressed that the articles written by Dai Zhen did not include any state secrets and that all the documents he forwarded with his articles were public. They denied providing Dai Zhen with a refrigerator or that he requested one from them and said that when he had occasionally asked them to buy him some daily necessities in Hong Kong, this was deducted from his wages. They also stated that it was normal that he should be paid monthly wages as he was a contributing editor to the magazine.

As stated earlier, Dai Zhen's trial was not held in public. According to Chinese law, cases which are found to involve "state secrets" can be held *in camera*.

The place where Dai Zhen is detained is not known and there has been no news of him since his trial in late 1982.

Father Vincent Zhu Hongsheng and other Catholic priests

Over 10 Roman Catholic priests and lay Catholics were arrested in Shanghai on 19 November 1981. They included Father Vincent Zhu Hongsheng, aged 70, and Fathers Stephen Chen Caijun, aged 66, Joseph Chen Yuntang, aged 76, Fu Hezhou, aged 71, George Huang Huaquan, aged 66, Stanislas Shen Baishun, aged 80, Stanislas Yan Yunliang, aged 66, Matthew Zhang Xibin, aged 74, and Francis Xavier Zhu Shude, aged 68. Also arrested were lay Catholics Joseph Zhu Yude, aged 52, and Matthew Zhu Lide, aged 50.

They were arrested, it is believed, because of their persistent refusal to cooperate with the government-sponsored Chinese Patriotic Catholic Association, and their continued loyalty to the Vatican. They were described in some press reports as "loyal Catholics", in contrast to the "patriotic Catholics" (i.e. members of the Patriotic Catholic Association). It was reported that they had celebrated mass and given baptism in private homes with authorization from Rome but independently of the official Chinese Catholic Church.

No official charges were made public at the time of their arrest in November 1981. Their arrest was, however, acknowledged in various official reports. On 13 December 1981, for instance, a senior Party official, Zhang Zhiyi, said that "it was fully correct to hit at counter-revolutionaries hidden in religious circles" and spoke of the "illegal activities" of "a few counter-revolutionaries and bad elements in the cloak of religion". At the same meeting, the Vice-President of the Patriotic Catholic Association, Bishop Louis Zhang Jiashu, noted that the "judicial departments had punished a few persons who had been released after serving their prison terms but had continued to engage in illegal activities under the cloak of Catholicism" (New China News Agency, 13 December 1981). Later, a leading member of the official Chinese Catholic Church, Bishop Michael Yang Gaojian, was also reported to have said: "Not long ago, the Chinese Government arrested Zhu Hongsheng and other counter-revolutionaries in religious clothing according to law. We deem it a good thing to bring these pharisees to justice to purify the Church." (New China News Agency, 19 March 1983).

Several of those arrested in November 1981 had previously been arrested on 8 September 1955 at the same time as the Bishop of Shanghai, Gong Pinmei, who is still detained after nearly 30 years in prison (see p. 19). They included Father Zhu Hongsheng, Father Chen Yuntang, Father Zhang Xibin, Joseph Zhu Yude and Matthew Zhu Lide. They were brought to trial in 1960 together with Bishop Gong and sentenced to long prison terms. They were released from their first period of imprisonment between 1977 and 1979 and returned to Shanghai. However, Father Zhu Hongsheng was almost alone in being granted a residence permit allowing him to live in Shanghai. The presence of the other priests in Shanghai was tolerated, but they were not legally allowed to reside there.

Father Vincent Zhu Hongsheng was sentenced to 15 years' imprisonment in 1960. His sentence would normally have expired in 1970, as sentences are generally served from the date of arrest. However, he was not released until 1979. After his release, he lived in Shanghai with his younger brother's family and it is reported that he received visitors from abroad, as he had many foreign friends and acquaintances. These included people whom he had met when studying in France and the USA during the 1940s. These connections with overseas visitors formed an important element in the charges brought against him at his trial. According to reports, on the day of his arrest 20 police officers searched his home from 9 am until midnight.

Four of the priests arrested in November 1981 are reported to have been tried in Shanghai in early 1983. They were apparently brought to trial in two separate groups. Father Zhu Hongsheng and Father Chen Yuntang were tried together and the verdict against them was reportedly announced on 22 March 1983. Zhu Hongsheng was sentenced to 15 years' imprisonment and Chen Yuntang to 11 years. According to information available to Amnesty International, the trial was not held openly, but about 100 people were officially invited to attend it; however, no family members were present. No official information or statement has been made public about the trial or verdict.

According to unofficial sources, the charges against Father Zhu Hongsheng and Father Chen Yuntang were: "colluding with foreign countries"; "endangering the sovereignty and security of the motherland"; "collecting intelligence reports"; "fabricating rumours"; and "carrying out incitement" or "subversive activities". These charges are believed to refer to the priests' contacts with foreign visitors, their continued allegiance to the Vatican and their independent religious activities. Father Zhu Hongsheng is reported to be held in Shanghai Prison No. 1, but no news of him has been received since the trial.

Father Stanislas Shen Baishun and Father Stephen Chen Caijun were tried earlier, either in February or early March 1983. Father Shen Baishun, who is 80 years old, was sentenced to 10 years' imprisonment and Father Chen Caijun to two and a half years' imprisonment. No official information has been made public about the trial or verdict and the precise charges against them are unknown. It is likely, however, that they were tried on charges similar to those brought against Fathers Zhu Hongsheng and Chen Yuntang. According to reports, Shen Baishun was transferred to a prison hospital in Shanghai some time after his trial as he suffers from a heart condition.

Another priest was reported to have been tried in mid-1983. According to reports, Father Francis Xavier Zhu Shude was tried in Chao Xian, Anhui province, and sentenced on 10 June 1983 to 12 years' imprisonment with deprivation of civil rights for an additional three years. No details of the trial have been officially made public. Father Zhu Shude had been first arrested in 1953 and was in fact still detained in a labour camp in Anhui province when the other priests were arrested in Shanghai in November 1981. It is reported that he had been allowed very occasionally to visit his mother in Shanghai. Apart from this, he remained confined to the labour camp. According to reports, he was tried and sentenced again in 1983 because he continued to carry out religious activities in the labour camp, including saying mass. Two of his brothers, Matthew Zhu Lide and Joseph Zhu Yude, were among those arrested in Shanghai in November 1981. They were reported to have been sent to labour camps in different provinces. Father Zhu Shude died in the labour camp in December 1983 after spending over 30 years in detention. He was aged 70 and is reported to have died of natural causes.

The circumstances and whereabouts of some of the other priests detained since 1981 remain unknown.

Thubten Kelsang Thalutsogentsang

Thubten Kelsang Thalutsogentsang, a 40-year-old former Tibetan monk and horse-cart driver, is reported to have been detained since 1981 for shouting slogans in favour of the independence of Tibet. He is reportedly held in Sangyip prison in Lhasa, in the Autonomous Region of Tibet.

According to information received by Amnesty International, Thubten Kelsang Thalutsogentsang was trained as a monk before his first arrest in 1959. Thousands of Tibetans were arrested at that period, following a rebellion against the occupation of Tibet by Chinese troops. How long he was imprisoned at that time is not known, but he is said to have been assigned to the Nachen corrective labour unit. He was reportedly kept under surveillance after his release, presumably because of his background as a monk, as in Tibet religion is often equated with independence and anti-Chinese feelings. Work "under surveillance" is a common form of punishment in China. It usually involves deprivation of certain rights, restriction of freedom of movement and the requirement that those concerned report regularly to the police or other local authorities.

Thubten Kelsang Thalutsogentsang then worked as horse-cart driver. He is reported to have been rearrested on 3 December 1981 in Lhasa for shouting slogans in favour of Tibet's independence. The precise circumstances of his arrest, however, are unknown. It is presumed that he shouted the slogans during a public meeting or event. Other Tibetans have been arrested in the past three years for shouting slogans in public or displaying posters in favour of independence. It was reported, for instance, that several people had been arrested for shouting such slogans during the visit to Tibet in

1980 of a delegation of Tibetan exiles representing the Dalai Lama.

It is not known whether Thubten Kelsang Thalutsogentsang has been tried and sentenced.

Liu Shanqing

Liu Shanqing, a 30-year-old computer sales engineer from Hong Kong, was arrested in the People's Republic of China when he went to Guangzhou for a short visit on 25 December 1981. He was due to stay there only two or three days and was expected to be back in Hong Kong by 28 December at the latest. However, he was arrested during his visit and has been imprisoned in China ever since. Liu Shanqing was a supporter of the "democracy movement" in China. During his trip to Guangzhou, he was planning to visit the relatives of two prisoners of conscience who had been detained there since April 1981.

His family in Hong Kong was not informed of his arrest and received no news of him for several months afterwards. On 13 March 1982 Liu Shanqing's father went to Guangzhou to ask the Chinese authorities about his son's whereabouts. It is reported that he was told by officials of Guangzhou Public Security Bureau that his son was under arrest, but no information was given to him about his son's whereabouts or the charges against him. He was also refused permission to visit him.

A committee for the "Rescue of Liu Shanqing", which was formed in Hong Kong by his friends, later received a letter from the Hong Kong Government which included a statement from the Chinese authorities. This was in response to an inquiry by the British Embassy in Beijing. The Chinese authorities reportedly stated that Liu Shanqing was considered by them to be a national of the People's Republic of China and that he was detained for "unlawful deeds". According to his family and friends, Liu Shanqing was born and brought up in Hong Kong. He studied at Hong Kong University and graduated from it in 1976. The People's Republic of China, however, considers that ethnic Chinese living in Hong Kong are citizens of the People's Republic of China.

Liu Shanqing's father is reported to have made two further trips from Hong Kong to Guangzhou—in June 1982 and March 1983— to find out why and where his son was detained. In March 1983 he was eventually told by officials of the Guangzhou Intermediate People's Court that his son had been tried and sentenced and that visits by relatives would be possible in about a month. However, he was not given any details of the trial or verdict and was simply told that instructions would be given to him later regarding visits. In a letter dated 10 August 1983 addressed to the Students' Union of the Chinese University of Hong Kong, which had campaigned for Liu's release, the Guangzhou Intermediate People's Court claimed that Liu Shanqing had been brought to a "public trial", although neither the family nor the friends of Liu Shanqing had been informed in advance of his trial despite repeated inquiries.

The court said in its letter that Liu had been collaborating with other "counter-revolutionary elements" to "attack the socialist system and the people's democratic dictatorship", to "carry out counter-revolutionary propaganda and agitation" and to "resist and violate the laws and regulations" of the country. He was convicted on these charges and sentenced to 10 years' imprisonment plus three years' deprivation of political rights according to Articles 50, 90 and 102 of the Criminal Law. The court further said that Liu Shanqing had appealed to Guangdong province High People's Court but that the original conviction and sentence had been upheld. It also said that Liu Shanqing's mother had visited him in prison.

Peter Joseph Fan Xueyan

The 76-year-old Roman Catholic Bishop of Baoding, Monsignor Peter Joseph Fan Xueyan, was reported in late 1983 to have been imprisoned for the second time and sentenced to 10 years' imprisonment for maintaining links with the Vatican and ordaining priests independently of the official Chinese Catholic Church.

Monsignor Fan Xueyan was one of the last Chinese bishops ordained by the Vatican in 1951, before the official Chinese Catholic Patriotic Association put pressure on the Chinese Church to break relations with Rome. Some priests who refused to join the association and remained loyal to the Pope were imprisoned.

Monsignor Fan was arrested for the first time in 1958 and sentenced to 15 years' imprisonment. According to a statement on 10 January 1984 by an official of the State Bureau of Religious Affairs, he was arrested then because of his opposition "to the Chinese Church's decision on its anti-imperialist, self-governing policy"; he "stubbornly refused to accept" the establishment of the Chinese Patriotic Catholic Association and he was "criticized by the Church and stripped of his post as bishop". Despite that, no other bishop was appointed while he was imprisoned and he was reinstated in the Baoding diocese after his release in 1979.

According to reports, Monsignor Fan was rearrested in March 1982 in Baoding together with the Vicar-General of Baoding,

Monsignor Huo Binzhang, aged 70, and some young priests and seminarists. It is also reported that some young people from Baoding had protested against his arrest at the time. Both Monsignor Fan and Monsignor Huo Binzhang were brought to trial in late 1983 and sentenced to 10 years' imprisonment. The State Bureau of Religious Affairs and the Chinese Foreign Ministry confirmed their trial and sentence in statements made on 10 January 1984.

According to these statements they were charged with "colluding with foreign forces to jeopardize the sovereignty and security of the motherland", an accusation which is believed to refer to their continued loyalty to the Vatican. No other details of their trial have been made public by the Chinese authorities.

Monsignor Huo Binzhang had himself been imprisoned previously. Both he and Monsignor Fan are said to be held at the Shijiazhuang prison in Hebei province.

The death penalty

The death penalty is used extensively in the People's Republic of China. The laws provide for it to be imposed as a punishment for a number of political offences, as well as for ordinary criminal offences. The crimes most often punished by death are murder, rape and robbery resulting in death or serious injury. However, since 1981 the number of offences carrying the death penalty has doubled, and people can now be executed for a wide range of offences, including theft, bribery, embezzlement, organizing a secret society, molesting women, gang fighting, drug trafficking, pimping or "passing on methods of committing crimes".

Legislation has been adopted on several occasions since 1982 not only to increase the number of offences punishable by death, but also to speed up proceedings in death penalty cases. The procedures for trial, appeal, review of sentence and execution have all been accelerated. Amnesty International expressed its concern in 1981 at the marked increase in the number of death sentences and executions after a decree was adopted which ended the review of all death sentences by the Supreme People's Court. Since then, other changes in legislation have resulted in further increases in the use of the death penalty. These amendments are described in detail in the following pages.

Other aspects of the use of the death penalty in China have been of concern to Amnesty International for many years. These include using "mass sentencing rallies" to publicize exemplary cases involving the death penalty; the authorities resorted to this practice particularly when they launched "law and order" campaigns throughout the country. The announcement of death sentences at such rallies has sometimes been shown on Chinese television. A rally attended by some 100,000 people in the northern city of Taiyuan was televised in July 1981. The rally was held to pronounce the verdict against 11 "top criminals", four of whom were sentenced to death. They were seen standing on army trucks, their heads bent by soldiers, facing the judges and prosecutors whose statements were

54

relayed by loudspeakers. After the verdict was pronounced they were driven immediately to the execution ground, but the execution was not shown on television.

A "mass sentencing rally" in Guilin, Yunnan province, 16 September 1983. The condemned prisoners, placards around their necks, stand on the trailer in the centre of the football stadium with their heads forced down. They are here to listen to their crimes being denounced before they are executed. Seated in front of the standing crowd are rows of uniformed soldiers. The trucks lined up at the rear of the stadium will be used to parade the prisoners through the streets of Guilin. Before the day is out, the prisoners will have been put to death.

Condemned prisoners are also frequently paraded in public before execution, and humiliated in other ways, such as by forcing them to keep their heads bowed. Such practices seem to contradict the spirit of the Law of Criminal Procedure adopted in 1979. Article 155 of that law states: "the execution of the death sentence should be announced, but the condemned should not be exposed to the public". Despite this provision, executions are still being carried out in public, according to both eye-witness accounts and foreign press reports.

In August 1983 the authorities launched a nation-wide campaign against crime. During the first three months of the campaign, tens of thousands of arrests and several thousand executions are believed to have been carried out. Amnesty International recorded more than 600 executions in only a few places in China during that period, and it believed that the total number of executions carried out throughout the country was far higher. Foreign press reports estimated the total number during the three months at over 5,000. According to a Hong Kong publication citing private conversations between Hong Kong intellectuals and Chinese jurists, over 10,000 people had been executed by January 1984. The rate of executions recorded at that time was the highest in China since the early 1970s.

Many of those executed were in groups of 15 to 40 people who were paraded in public in the streets or during mass rallies. They were then shot later that day. It was reported in one instance to Amnesty International that a group of condemned prisoners paraded in trucks through the streets of Nanjing in September 1983 showed signs of having been beaten, with bruises on their faces.

Condemned prisoners being paraded through the centre of Xining, Qinghai province, in August 1983. The soldiers in the truck force down the prisoners' heads; the placards round their necks announce the crimes for which they have been sentenced to death.

On 21 October 1983 Amnesty International wrote to President Li Xiannian calling for a halt to the wave of executions. The organization expressed concern about the repeated increases in the use of the death penalty over the previous few years. It noted in particular measures adopted on 2 September 1983 by the Standing Committee of the National People's Congress (NPC), China's supreme legislative body. These increased the number of offences punishable by death and accelerated the procedures for trial, appeal and execution in some cases involving the death penalty. The organization said that the speed with which trials and executions were being carried out under this legislation did not allow for the procedural safeguards for the death penalty to which the United Nations General Assembly had drawn attention several times. It also pointed out that the increased use of the death penalty contradicted the aim of rehabilitation acknowledged in Chinese law.

Amnesty International has received no direct reply from the Chinese authorities to its letter. However, on 2 November 1983 a spokesperson of the Chinese Foreign Ministry is reported to have acknowledged receipt of the letter and to have said: "Criminals must receive the punishment they deserve according to the law. This is a normal measure and routine work to maintain the public security of a country. It is the internal affair of a country."

Amnesty International is unconditionally opposed to the death penalty on the grounds that it is a violation of the right to life and the right not to be subjected to cruel, inhuman or degrading treatment or punishment as proclaimed in the Universal Declaration of Human Rights.

Legislation and practice

Offences punishable by the death penalty

On 1 July 1979 the Standing Committee of the National People's Congress adopted several laws including the Criminal Law and the Law of Criminal Procedure, both of which include provisions concerning the death penalty. They came into effect on 1 January 1980.

The Criminal Law then listed seven ordinary offences and 14 "counter-revolutionary" offences punishable by death, the latter when they are "of a particularly heinous nature causing grave harm to the people and state" (Article 103). These "counter-revolutionary" offences include "colluding with foreign countries to jeopardize the security of the motherland" (Article 91), "plotting to overthrow the government and split the country" (Article 92), incitement to defection or rebellion (Article 93), defection (Article 94), organizing "armed rebellious assemblies" or jailbreaks (Articles 95 and 96), espionage (Article 97) and various acts of "sabotage" to public buildings or installations, hijacking and stealing weapons and ammunitions (Article 100). The death penalty may also be imposed for "deliberate homicide" (Article 132), rape "when the victim is seriously wounded or killed" (Article 139), stealing in circumstances causing "injury or the death of any person" (Article 150), and embezzlement in "extremely grave cases" (Article 155). Before the

Criminal Law was adopted, most of the "counter-revolutionary" offences listed above and "serious cases" of corruption or counterfeiting state currency were already punishable by death under laws adopted in 1951 and 1952. There was, however, no legislation to cover the ordinary offences, although murder had traditionally been punishable by death.

Since 1981 new legislation has been adopted introducing the death penalty for a further 23 offences. This legislation includes the following measures:

a) Provisional Regulations adopted by the National People's Congress Standing Committee on 10 June 1981 provide the death penalty as an alternative punishment for 10 categories of military offence. These are: providing military secrets to enemies or foreigners; threats or violence against army personnel on duty; theft of weapons or equipment; sabotage; spreading rumours undermining army morale; desertion; disobedience; making false reports; assisting the enemy after surrendering; robbing and harming civilians.

These regulations state that they are intended primarily to punish army personnel who commit "offences against their duties". Several of their provisions are applicable in time of both peace and war, while others are applicable only in wartime. They codify as law what were previously military regulations. This decree (the full title of which is "Provisional Regulations of the PRC on Punishing Servicemen Who Commit Offences Against Their Duties") came into force on 1 January 1982.

b) An amendment to the Criminal Law adopted on 8 March 1982 provides heavier punishments, including the death penalty, for economic crimes such as smuggling, bribery, theft, drug-trafficking, speculation and the illegal export of valuable cultural relics. The adoption of this measure was part of a campaign to eradicate corruption among state officials. In a commentary published on 10 March 1982 the official newspaper the *People's Daily* said:

"The government and the Party have always advocated using capital punishment as little as possible but the shocking incidence of economic crimes has reached such proportions that they must be seriously punished. A small minority of extremely serious criminals must be punished by means of the ultimate penalty in order to serve as a warning to others."

The amendment came into force on 1 April 1982. When it was adopted, the official Chinese press announced that those guilty of economic offences who confessed voluntarily before 1 May 1982 would be treated leniently. By 20 April, nearly 3,000 people had confessed to economic crimes, according to the official press. By the end of 1982 no death sentences or executions for economic offences had been reported, but several high-ranking Chinese officials were being detained for investigation on charges of "large-scale smuggling". The first executions reported to have been carried out under this amendment took place in January 1983. One of those executed was Wang Zhong, a 56-year-old official from Haifang in Guangdong province, who was convicted of corruption by the Intermediate People's Court of Shantou and executed on 17 January 1983. He was accused of embezzling the equivalent of £20,000 in goods seized from smugglers and of accepting bribes. Wang was head of the anti-smuggling brigade and secretary of Haifang county Communist Party committee, as well as deputy head of Shantou political and judicial committee. The New China News Agency reported that this was the first execution for corruption since the government had begun cracking down on economic crimes. Wang's appeal to the provincial High People's Court was turned down and his sentence was approved by the Supreme People's Court. The New China News Agency said that the *People's Daily* would carry an editorial the following day hailing the punishment "as good news most gratifying to the people".

c)   Further amendments to the Criminal Law were introduced on 2 September 1983 when the National People's Congress Standing Committee took a "Decision on Severely Punishing Criminals Who Gravely Endanger Public Security".* Seven new categories of offence were made liable to the death penalty, bringing to over 40

---

* The decision was specifically directed against the following people:

"(1) The ringleader of a criminal gang or anyone who engages in serious gangster activities with a lethal weapon or whose gangster activities are particularly dangerous; (2) Anyone who commits intentional assault and battery and causes severe injury or death to another person in an absolutely vile way, or engages in violence and causes injury to policemen or citizens who report, expose and arrest criminals and stop criminal activities; (3) The ringleader of a group engaging in abduction for purposes of trafficking in human beings or anyone who abducts in a particularly serious way; (4) Anyone who illegally makes, or trades, transports or steals weapons, ammunition or explosives in a particularly serious way or with serious consequences; (5) Anyone who organizes reactionary secret societies or sects and utilizes feudal superstitious beliefs to carry out counter-revolutionary activities and gravely endangers public security; (6) Anyone who lures, houses or forces a female to engage in prostitution and whose case is particularly grave; (7) Anyone who passes on methods of committing crimes, (. . .) in a particularly grave case, (. . .) will be sentenced to life imprisonment or death."

the total number of offences now punishable by death. The officially stated aim of this measure was to clamp down on criminal gangs, "hardened hooligans" and habitual offenders. Wang Hanbin, Secretary General of the Standing Committee, explained the need for the new legislation as follows:

"The 'Criminal Law' stipulates that the death penalty may be imposed on criminals involved in homicide, rape, robbery, explosions and other activities that seriously threaten public safety. These serious criminal offenders should be severely punished in accordance with the law. At the same time, we must note that some offenders who committed serious crimes, did grave harm to society, and incurred the greatest popular indignation in the past few years have escaped the death penalty because of relevant articles in the 'Criminal Law'. In the light of these crimes, it is necessary to revise and supplement the law. . . .

"'Only by resolutely striking at criminals who have seriously threatened public safety can we frighten the offenders, frustrate their arrogance, protect the life and property of the broad masses of people, educate and help minor criminals to mend their ways, and strive for a fundamental change for the better in public order and ensure the smooth building of the four modernizations."

(New China News Agency, 2 September 1983)

These amendments to the Criminal Law further broadened the range of offences punishable by death. The new offences included assault and battery, organizing a "counter-revolutionary" secret society, stealing or trafficking in weapons or ammunitions, pimping, abduction for the purpose of trafficking in human beings, gang fighting, molesting women, and "passing on methods of committing crimes."

A wave of mass executions marked the "campaign against crime" for which these amendments were introduced. It started even before the amendments had been adopted. On 23 August 1983, 30 people were executed in Beijing following a mass rally of an estimated 100,000 people. The 29 men and one woman were said to be between 18 and 24 years old, with most of them being around 20. They had been sentenced by Beijing High People's Court. Nineteen were convicted of murder, 10 of rape and one of theft. After their execution, their photographs were displayed outside a court building, as well as those of 15 other people who had been executed some time before in the capital. Executions were then reported in various Chinese cities on 30 August and 1 September 1983, including those of five members

A "criminal element" being arrested by a police officer: detail from a poster in the campaign against crime launched in August 1983.

of a "gang of robbers" convicted of injuring people in an attempted robbery in Shanghai.

Executions of groups of 15 to 40 people continued during the following months throughout the country. Many of those executed were reported to have been unemployed young people aged between 18 and 40. While most of those executed appeared to have been convicted of murder, rape or robbery, people were also executed for a wide range of other offences. For example, two men were executed in Guangzhou on 5 September 1983 after being convicted of hanging a banner with a "counter-revolutionary" slogan from a hotel window and of plotting to set up a radio station and two subversive organizations. Two other men were executed on 24 September 1983 in Tianjin after being convicted of organizing a traditional-style secret society based on ancient rituals and religious practices. A peasant was executed in Shanghai on 12 September for "molesting women" and two men in Guangdong on 26 October after being convicted of stealing antiques from a museum.

With the amendments to the Criminal Law introduced on 2 September 1983, several other measures were adopted by the National People's Congress to accelerate the procedures for trial, appeal and execution (see below). The "Decision on Severely Punishing Criminals who Gravely Endanger Public Security" took effect on the day of its adoption and applied immediately to relevant criminal trials. As a result, people were tried under the new legislation for offences allegedly committed before this legislation was adopted. For example, four men—Cheng Jian, Xie Yinbin, Peng Zijun and Yin Qingjiang—were executed on 4 September 1983 in Shumchun in front of hundreds of onlookers. They had been convicted of robbing a major store in July 1983 in Guangdong province. Before the Criminal Law was amended on 2 September 1983, robbery or stealing was liable to the death penalty only when it was committed in circumstances causing "injury or the death of any person".

This use of legislation contravenes the principle that laws must not be applied retroactively, a principle firmly established in international human rights standards. In particular, Article 6(2) of the International Covenant on Civil and Political Rights states that a "sentence of death may be imposed only . . . in accordance with the law in force at the time of the commission of the crime." Article 11(2) of the Universal Declaration of Human Rights states:

> "No one shall be held guilty of any penal offence on account of any act or omission which did not constitute a penal offence, under national or international law, at the time when it was committed. Nor shall a heavier penalty be imposed than the one that was applicable at the time the

The court notice giving details of the death sentence is usually posted on the day of the execution. The large red tick shows that the victim has already been executed. Nanjing, Jiangsu province, 30 September 1983.

penal offence was committed.''

The repeated increases in the number of offences punishable by death also contradicts the principles established in a resolution adopted on 8 December 1977 by the United Nations General Assembly. This resolution states:

"The General Assembly, . . .

i. Reaffirms that, as established by the General Assembly in resolution 2857 (XXVI) and by the Economic and Social Council in resolutions 1574 (L), 1745 (LIV) and 1930 (LVIII), the main objective to be pursued in the field of capital punishment is that of progressively restricting the number of offences for which the death penalty may be imposed with a view to the desirability of abolishing this punishment''

(United Nations General Assembly resolution 32/61)

A full list of the articles of Chinese law providing for the death penalty is included in Appendix C.

Restrictions

The only restriction on the use of the death penalty applies to pregnant women and to children. Article 44 of the Criminal Law states that the death penalty is not "suitable" for pregnant women and minors (under the age of 18 at the time of the crime). However, the same article also stipulates that "a person between 16 and 18 years of age who has committed a particularly serious offence may be sentenced to death with a two-year reprieve".

The official Chinese news media recently publicized the case of a lawyer who was arrested and detained by local officials when he tried to have his client's case reviewed. After his client had been sentenced to death, the lawyer received what he believed to be evidence that his client was not yet 18. Although this information was reportedly false, the lawyer did not know that. Shortly after asking for a review of the case he was arrested on the orders of the public prosecutor's office and accused of aiding and abetting the defendant. His house was then ransacked and he was detained for more than a month before his case was heard. The official news media publicized the case as an example of the lack of respect for the law on the part of some officials.

Suspended death sentences

In addition to those death sentences which are designated as being "for immediate execution" it is possible for the courts to pronounce a death sentence in which execution is suspended for two years. This system has existed since 1949 and is now maintained in the Criminal Law. In such cases, offenders have to carry out "reform through labour" during the period of reprieve and their attitudes are examined to see if they show "evidence of repentance". If the offender is considered to show repentance, the sentence may be commuted at the end of the two-year reprieve to life imprisonment or a fixed term of imprisonment. If it is found that he or she "seriously resists reform" the death sentence will be carried out (Article 46). Article 47 specifies that the period of reprieve of the death sentence is effective from the date of sentencing.

Very little information is available on the procedure used to assess the behaviour of condemned offenders during the period of reprieve and the proportion of sentences commuted at the end of the two years is not known. When the new laws which came into effect on 1 January 1980 were adopted by the National People's Congress in July 1979, Sha Qianli, an official of the Legal Affairs Commission of the NPC, commented as follows on China's "unique institution" of granting those sentenced to death a two-year reprieve:

"Generally speaking, those receiving the reprieve will not be executed as long as they do not refuse in a particularly serious manner to mend their ways. If a criminal shows real signs of repentance and performs meritorious service, his sentence may be commuted to life imprisonment or to a term of not less than 15 years and no more than 20 years.

"Practice has shown that the reprieve of the death sentence, by applying revolutionary humanism and trying in every way to retrieve the convicts, is a good way to make criminals turn over a new leaf. While educating law offenders, the criminal law especially forbids any insult to their personal dignity and forbids corporal punishment. Any judicial worker who violates this principle will be punished by law. Damage to the prisoners' minimum self respect does not help them turn over a new leaf and transform themselves ideologically."

(New China News Agency, 6 July 1979)

According to the law, officials of the penal institution where the prisoner spends the two years of reprieve are responsible for submitting to the relevant high people's court a written report on the prisoner at the end of the period of reprieve. If the prisoner is found to have "shown repentance" satisfactorily, the high court may commute the death sentence. If the offender is found to have "resisted reform" and execution is recommended, the high court must itself submit a report to the Supreme People's Court for approval before execution. (Law of Criminal Procedure, Article 153).

The best known examples of death sentences passed with a two-year reprieve are those in the cases of Jiang Qing (Mao Zedong's widow) and Zhang Chunqiao, two members of the so-called "Gang of Four". They were convicted of various "counter-revolutionary" offences and given suspended death sentences in January 1981. On 25 January 1983, the Supreme People's Court commuted the death sentences to life imprisonment. According to press reports, the Supreme People's Court said that the commutations were made "in view of their behaviour during the period of reprieve" and that an examination had shown that "the two criminals had not resisted reform in a flagrant way".

The number of people currently under a suspended death sentence is not known. Few cases of death sentences with reprieve have been reported since mid-1983. There are, however, indications that there may be many. Following the wave of mass executions which started in August 1983, An Zhiquo, the political editor of the official English-language weekly *Beijing Review*, wrote in an editorial on capital punishment:

"So far, only a small number of felons have been executed. (. . .) Many other criminals who also deserve the death

sentence but have shown repentance have been sentenced to
death with reprieve.''

(*Beijing Review*, 7 November 1983)

Trial procedure

There are three levels of courts corresponding to different administrative divisions in China: the Basic, Intermediate and High People's
Courts. At the national level, the country also has a Supreme
People's Court. The Intermediate and High People's Courts both
have jurisdiction to try cases punishable by death.

Little is known about the procedure followed at the trials of
people sentenced to death, apart from what is revealed by published
legislation or by the official accounts of such cases. Public notices
summarizing the cases of condemned offenders are usually posted
outside the buildings of the courts which passed the sentences. Such
notices are written by the courts and signed by the courts' presidents.
For offenders sentenced to death without reprieve, the notices are
usually posted on the day of the execution and often a tick in red
ink indicates that the execution has taken place. Although they
include some biographical data about the condemned offenders,
these notices usually give no information about the procedures followed at the trials. Various forms of ''mass public trials'' are also
organized by the courts and local officials to announce the sentences
passed on offenders. However, these are large gatherings—often
involving thousands of participants—rather than trials, and they are
aimed at publicizing the cases and at inviting the public to participate
in denouncing the accused.

There is, therefore, little official information on the actual proceedings followed in capital trials. According to private sources,
however, such proceedings are very summary when a ''law and
order'' campaign is under way. Although the right to defence is in
principle guaranteed by law, in practice the possibilities of exercising
this right effectively are small. Several of the minimum guarantees
for a fair trial spelt out in the International Covenant on Civil and
Political Rights (Article 14)* appear not to be respected. These
include the right to adequate time and facilities to prepare the
defence and the right to cross-examine prosecution witnesses and to
call witnesses for the defence. Furthermore, there is no recognition
—either in law or in practice—of the right to be presumed innocent
before being proved guilty in a court of law.

Such trends have been confirmed recently by the adoption on 2

* The text of Article 14 is given in Appendix D.

September 1983 of a "Decision of the NPC Standing Committee on the Procedure to Swiftly Try Criminals who Seriously Jeopardize Public Security". The decision, which came into force immediately, applied to cases of homicide, rape, robbery, explosions and "other activities that seriously threaten public security". Other cases liable to the death penalty would still be tried according to previous legislation.

The decision specified that the "criminals" accused of the offences listed above "who warrant the death penalty *should be tried swiftly if the major facts of the crime are clear, the evidence is conclusive and they have incurred great popular indignation*" (emphasis added) —in other words, if there is a presumption of guilt before the trial. In order to speed up trial procedures in such cases, this decision allowed the courts to bring defendants to trial without giving them a copy of the indictment in advance, and without giving advance notice of the trial or serving summonses in advance to all parties involved. Such advance notification had previously been required by the Law of Criminal Procedure (Article 110). The decision also specified that the time limit for appeals against a judgment had been reduced from 10 to three days.

As indicated by its title and text, the aim of the decision was "to swiftly and severely punish criminals who seriously jeopardize public security and to safeguard the interests of the state and the people". No time limit on its application was specified when it was adopted and it remained in force in mid-1984.

Appeal and review

According to the Law of Criminal Procedure (as promulgated in January 1980) the accused has the right to one appeal. If there is no appeal by the defendant, a death sentence passed by an Intermediate People's Court will be automatically reviewed by a High People's Court. The court of second instance should then review the case within one month or at most one month and a half. When it came into force, the Law of Criminal Procedure stated also that all death sentences have to be approved by the Supreme People's Court. As will be seen, this provision has since been changed.

Successful appeals are rare. The following is the only case to have come to Amnesty International's attention in recent years. In late 1980, Beijing radio reported that the Supreme People's Court had quashed a death sentence passed by a local court when it was reviewing it for approval. Details of the case had first been given by Shenyang Radio (Liaoning province) on 30 April 1980—the day on which the defendants were brought to a "public trial" by Shenyang Intermediate People's Court. The defendants, Guan Qingchang, a cadre in a factory, and his wife, were convicted of embezzling more than 40 kilogrammes of gold 19 years earlier at the factory. They had been arrested in April 1980 when they reportedly tried to sell part of the gold. Guan Qingchang was sentenced to death by the Intermediate People's Court and his wife was given a two-year suspended death sentence. It was announced at their trial that they would appeal to the provisional High People's Court if they did not agree with the verdict. The High People's Court, however, approved the verdict passed by the intermediate court and submitted the case to the Supreme People's Court for approval. On 6 November 1980 Beijing radio reported that the Supreme People's Court had quashed the judgment. The Committee of Judges of the Supreme People's Court had determined that although Guan Qingchang was a government official he had not used his authority to commit the crime, and his wife was not a government official. Further, the selling in April 1980 of the stolen gold was only a continuation of the act of theft committed in 1961. They ruled that the crime was not one of embezzlement but of theft—a lesser crime at the time—and referred the case back to Liaoning High People's Court for reappraisal. After reviewing the case, the High People's Court decided on 11 November 1980 to commute the death sentences passed by the Intermediate People's Court. Guan Qingchang's sentence was commuted to life imprisonment with deprivation of political rights for life, and his wife's sentence was commuted to 10 years' imprisonment.

In another case reported in 1980, an appeal by the defendant resulted in his original sentence of 15 years' imprisonment being changed to a death sentence suspended for two years. The defendant, Wang Li, together with a co-defendant, Meng Xiaohong, had first been tried for corruption and embezzlement by Beijing Intermediate People's Court on 22 January 1980. He then appealed to Beijing High People's Court but, after hearing the case, the High Court ruled that the penalties were inappropriate and ordered that the case be retried by the intermediate court. At the retrial on 30 May 1980, the sentences were increased. This appears to violate the Law of Criminal Procedure which states that a court of second instance should not increase the penalty on a defendant on appeal.* According to a report by the New China News Agency on 30 May 1980, the court maintained that:

"because the defendant Wang Li abused his power to embezzle a huge sum of money from the state and the

* Article 137 says: "In its judgment of a case based on an appeal by the accused . . ., the people's court of second instance shall not aggravate the punishment originally imposed on the accused."

defendant Meng Xiaohong actively colluded in these crimes, the nature of their crime was serious, the way in which the crimes were committed was vile and their disgusting conduct would have a very bad influence. To protect state property from being violated and guarantee the smooth progress of the four modernizations, it was imperative that stiffer sentences be given to the two defendants."

However, sentences are rarely either reduced or increased on appeal or review and the trend in recent years has been towards curtailing such procedures even further.

The 2 September 1983 decision of the National People's Congress Standing Committee on "swiftly trying criminals" reduced the time limit for appeals from 10 to three days. At the same time, the Standing Committee adopted a decision to amend the "Organic Law of the People's Courts of the PRC". This amendment allowed the Supreme People's Court to delegate its power to approve death sentences in cases of murder, rape, robbery, use of explosives and "other cases seriously endangering public security and social order". The approval of death sentences in these cases could be delegated to high courts of provinces or courts of the equivalent level.

Another major amendment to the Organic Law of the People's Courts removed from Article 4 the statement that the courts "exercise their judicial authority independently" and are "subordinate only to the law", replacing it by a clause which, though it prevents the intervention of "administrative" authorities in the court's work does not specifically prevent that of political authorities. Article 4 was revised to read: "The people's courts exercise their judicial authority according to law and are independent of intervention by administrative organizations, social bodies and individuals."

When the amendments were adopted, Wang Hanbin, Secretary General of the National People's Congress Standing Committee, explained that they were necessary because if the original provisions of the Law of Criminal Procedure were applied to such cases . . .

". . . we shall not be able to try swiftly some cases that need to be tried right away, thus hindering our efforts to frighten the criminals, frustrate their arrogance, maintain public order and protect the life and property of the people. These criminals differ from counter-revolutionaries, embezzlers and other offenders in general in that the evidence of the crime can be easily and quickly obtained and some are caught on the spot; therefore they can be tried swiftly without a mix-up of cases."

(New China News Agency, 2 September 1983)

The decision allowing the Supreme People's Court to delegate its approval of death sentences to the high courts was in fact merely extending a similar decree adopted in June 1981. This decree, however, had been adopted as a provisional measure, for the period from 1981 to the end of 1983. Its stated aim was to reduce a backlog of cases awaiting judgment by the Supreme Court. The adoption of the decree in June 1981 was followed by a marked increase in the number of executions reported to have been carried out. In his comments on the amendments adopted on 2 September 1983, Wang Hanbin referred as follows to the usefulness of the 1981 decree and the need to incorporate it as a permanent measure:

"This has proved to be very necessary to strike at and deter criminal offenders and to safeguard social order and security. Facts upon which the death penalty is meted out are relatively clear and mistakes in meting such a penalty can not easily occur. It is necessary to uphold this decision under the present circumstances in which social security is still a serious problem."

(New China News Agency, 2 September 1983)

After these measures had been adopted, a man named Chen Guangsen was reported to have been executed only eight days after his alleged offence. He was executed in Guangzhou on 12 September 1983. Two young men—Cao Guorong and Xu Xianping—aged only 18 and 19 were officially reported to have been executed just six days after the crime for which they were convicted. According to a public notice about their case from Nanjing's Intermediate People's Court, they were arrested on 4 September 1983 in Nanjing and executed on 10 September 1983. The court notice indicates that the High People's Court of Jiangsu province had also reviewed the case and approved the verdict within the six days between their arrest and execution.

Amnesty International is concerned that the rapidity with which trials and executions are carried out under this legislation does not allow for the internationally accepted safeguards in death penalty cases which the United Nations General Assembly has stressed several times. In particular General Assembly Resolution 35/172 of 15 December 1980 on Arbitrary or Summary Executions states that the most careful legal procedures and the greatest possible safeguards for the accused must be guaranteed in capital cases and urges member states "to respect as a minimum standard the content of the provisions of Articles 6, 14 and 15 of the International Covenant on Civil and Political Rights." The text of these articles is given in Appendix D.

In a letter addressed to President Li Xiannian on 21 October 1983

The red tick on the text indicates that the two men have been executed. They were put to death within one week of the crime for which they were condemned.

Summary translation of a *Public Notice from Nanjing Intermediate People's Court*, dated 10 September 1983, on the cases of Cao Guorong and Xu Xianping:

Thief of guns and ammunition and murderer *Cao Guorong*, male, 18 years old, from Shaoxing in Zhejiang province. A worker in a factory in Nanjing, he had been assigned to carry out "re-education-through-labour" for one year in June 1982 for theft.

Co-accused *Xu Xianping*, male, 19 years old, from Zhejiang province, a worker in the same factory in Nanjing.

The criminal Cao Guorong and Xu Xianping plotted together to steal some guns. On 4 September, after they held secret talks to plan some action, the criminal Cao took advantage of the fact that his brother (who is a policeman) was sleeping in the house to steal his brother's model "64" pistol and five cartridges. Then, at around 10 o'clock in the evening, they went to Nanjing Railway station, with the intention of making a surprise attack on the Public Security office to steal guns, and then flee. When the policeman on duty became suspicious of Cao's movements and started interrogating him, the criminal Cao unexpectedly fired at him with his gun but the policeman seized the gun and forced him to the ground. The two criminals Cao and Xu struggled with the stolen guns and continued to resist arrest, but they were finally beaten down and captured on the spot by the police who brought them to justice.

The criminal Cao Guorong and Xu Xianping stole weapons and opened fire to resist arrest. The circumstances of their case are particularly grave. Thus, in order to seriously punish criminals who gravely endanger public safety and engage in major criminal activities, and in order to maintain public order, this court has condemned to death the criminals Cao Guorong and Xu Xianping who stole guns and ammunition and committed murder, and has deprived them of political rights for life, according to Articles 112, 132 and 53 of the PRC Criminal Law and in keeping with the sixth session of the NPC Standing Committee "Decision to Swiftly Punish Criminals Who Seriously Jeopardize Public Security". After the High People's Court of Jiangsu province approved the death sentence and ordered it to be carried out, this court had the criminals escorted today to the place of execution, where they were shot.

(signed by the Court President)
10 September 1983

Amnesty International noted:

> "The importance of procedural safeguards is all the greater because of the irreversible nature of the death penalty: once an innocent person is executed, the error can never be corrected. Yet the current trend in the People's Republic of China would appear to be towards curtailing such safeguards."

In particular, the following safeguards would appear not to be guaranteed in China, except for the right to review by a higher tribunal:

> "... It ... follows from the express terms of Article 6 that it [the death penalty] can only be imposed in accordance with the law in force at the time of the commission of the crime and not contrary to the Covenant. The procedural guarantees therein prescribed must be observed, including the right to a fair hearing by an independent tribunal, the presumption of innocence, the minimum guarantees for the defence, and the right to review by a higher tribunal. These rights are applicable in addition to the particular right to seek pardon or commutation of the sentence."

> (General Comment on Article 6 of the International Covenant on Civil and Political Rights, adopted at its 378th meeting [16th session] on 27 July 1982 by the Human Rights Committee set up under the Covenant)

Clemency

When the fourth constitution of the People's Republic of China was adopted by the National People's Congress on 4 December 1982, the post of State President which had been abolished during the Cultural Revolution was reinstated. According to Article 80 of the new constitution, the President has the power to issue pardons —and therefore to commute death sentences—though in doing so he must act upon the decision of the Standing Committee of the National People's Congress.

However, no appeals for clemency to the President have been reported since the constitution was adopted and the existing legislation does not contain any provisions permitting defendants to make such appeals.

In its Resolution 35/172 of 15 December 1980, the United Nations General Assembly urged member states:

> "(b) To examine the possibility of making automatic the

72

appeal procedure, where it exists, in cases of death sentences, as well as the consideration of an amnesty, pardon or commutation in these cases"

Article 6 of the International Covenant on Civil and Political Rights also states:

"Anyone sentenced to death shall have the right to seek pardon or commutation of the sentence. Amnesty, pardon or commutation of the sentence of death may be granted in all cases."

Execution

Article 45 of the Criminal Law states that execution is by firing-squad.

When a death sentence "to be executed immediately" is pronounced or approved by the Supreme People's Court, the President of the court should sign an order to carry out the death sentence (Article 153 of the Law of Criminal Procedure). Article 154 specifies that after being issued, the order should be carried out within seven days, except "(1) if it is discovered before the death sentence is carried out that the sentence might be wrong; (2) if it is discovered that the condemned person is pregnant". Amnesty International believes that the lack of time between review and execution, together with summary trial proceedings, increases the possibilities of error.

Furthermore, the procedure requiring the Supreme People's Court's approval before execution no longer applies in all cases. The provincial or equivalent high courts now have the power to order execution in some cases. The official accounts often do not even indicate whether death sentences passed by Intermediate People's Courts have been reviewed and approved by the high courts. During the wave of mass executions which started in August 1983, people were tried summarily and executed within a very short space of time. It would appear unlikely that proper appeal procedures could have been carried out in many cases.

Article 155 of the Law of Criminal Procedure states that the following procedures should be followed for carrying out a death sentence:

"Before carrying out a death sentence, the People's Court should notify the People's Procuratorate to send an official to supervise the execution.

"The judicial personnel directing the execution should examine and verify the identity of the condemned, ask him if he has any last words or letters and then turn him over to the executioner to be executed. If before the execution it is discovered that there might be a mistake, the execution should be suspended temporarily, and a report should be submitted to the Supreme People's Court for a ruling.

"The execution of the death sentence should be announced, but the condemned should not be exposed to the public.

"After the execution, the court clerk present should make proper note of it.

"The People's Court that had the death sentence carried out should submit a report on the execution to the Supreme People's Court.

"After the execution, the People's Court that had the death sentence carried out should notify the family members of the condemned."

Public executions were carried out in China before 1980, particularly at times of political tension. They usually took place at the end of mass rallies held in stadiums or similar public places. A particularly large number of public executions was carried out during a "law and order" campaign at the end of 1979, before the new laws came into force in January 1980. Executions have even been televised. The execution of Xiong Ziping, one of two twin brothers from Hangzhou convicted of rape, was shown on television in Beijing on 17 November 1979. In a report on the trial on 8 November 1979, the New China News Agency stated that the authorities in Hangzhou urged various organizations "to use this typical case as negative material in the current publicity on the legal system". Xiong Ziping was sentenced to death on 14 November. According to Hangzhou radio, "after the trial, Xiong Ziping was executed immediately by armed police at the execution ground." Part of the trial and the execution were shown on television in Beijing three days later. According to various accounts Xiong Ziping was forced to kneel by three armed police officers standing behind him while a fourth held a rifle. Then Xiong Ziping was shown collapsing forward to the ground after being shot.

Xiong Ziping's execution appears to be typical. The victims are forced to kneel by two or three soldiers or police officers standing behind them. Their hands are usually tied behind their back. They are then shot in the back of the head by one of the soldiers or police officers. This practice is inherited from Imperial China when the executioner traditionally avoided facing his victim for fear that the victim's soul might later come and haunt him.

Public executions were supposed to have stopped with the promulgation of the Law of Criminal Procedure in January 1980. However, despite the provisions of Article 155 that "the execution of the

An execution. The victim listens to the judgment against him. Forced to his knees, he will, within minutes, be shot in the back of the head. These photographs were publicly displayed in the streets of Kunming, Yunnan province, in late July 1982.

death sentence should be announced, but the condemned should not be exposed to the public'', it is reported that some executions are still being carried out in public and the prisoners' bodies exposed to the public afterwards. The *Washington Post* of 20 January 1984 cited Japanese reporters touring Anhui province in December 1983 who had arrived at an execution ground where the bodies of 10 men who had just been shot were surrounded by 2,000 people; among them ''the executioner was standing with a cigarette in one hand and a pistol in the other . . . It was a grisly scene.''

Posthumous rehabilitation

Executions have later been officially recognized to have been mistaken in some rare cases. Zhang Zhixin, a 45-year-old woman, was executed for her political opinions in 1975. Information about her became available from official sources in 1979, when she was rehabilitated as a ''revolutionary martyr''. Although nothing had been reported about her case previously, in 1979 it became the focus of a major press campaign in China to highlight the crimes committed under the ''Gang of Four'' and their followers.

Before her arrest in 1969 Zhang Zhixin had been a cadre in the Bureau of Literature and Art attached to the Party Committee's Propaganda Department of Liaoning province. Her views on Chinese political affairs became known to her colleagues in 1968. She was reportedly critical of Lin Biao (the former Defence Minister who disappeared after an alleged coup attempt in 1971) and of Jiang Qing (Mao Zedong's wife, now stigmatized as the ''chief culprit'' in the ''Gang of Four''). As Zhang Zhixin maintained her views despite attending a ''reform-study class'', she was arrested as an ''active counter-revolutionary'' in September 1969. Brought to trial in 1974, she was first sentenced to life imprisonment but then secretly retried and sentenced to death "for immediate execution" on 3 April 1975. With no time left for appeal, she was executed that very day in the provincial prison where she was held.

According to reports published in 1979 by unofficial Chinese journals, her throat was cut before her execution to prevent her from shouting slogans. During the Cultural Revolution such practices were reportedly used to prevent condemned political offenders from yelling revolutionary slogans such as "Long live the Chinese Communist Party" or "Long live Chairman Mao" before they were shot. The method used on Zhang Zhixin is alleged to have been invented by a forensic specialist from Shenyang Prison (Liaoning province) during the Cultural Revolution. He allegedly carried out operations without anaesthetics on 60 people, including Zhang Zhixin.

A campaign of propaganda about her case followed her rehabilitation in March 1979. It appears to have been primarily aimed against high-ranking regional officials held responsible for her death, who were denounced as "followers" of the "Gang of Four". Her case also occasioned some debate on the legal system at a time when new laws were being drafted and the Chinese news media were emphasizing the need to respect legal procedures. There was little comment, however, on the death penalty itself, even though her treatment before execution caused a public outcry and her execution was labelled not only a "mistake" but, in fact, a crime.

Also officially acknowledged as a "mistake" was the execution of Wang Shenyou in 1977. Shanghai radio reported on 3 April 1981 that the Shanghai Party Committee had held a meeting on that day to rehabilitate Wang Shenyou, a student who was reportedly persecuted during the Cultural Revolution for opposing Lin Biao and the "Gang of Four". Wang was arrested on 10 September 1976 and executed on 27 April 1977. At the request of his family in 1979, the Shanghai High People's Court re-examined the case and found that the death sentence passed on Wang Shenyou was "a mistake". He was "pronounced not guilty" and "his reputation was restored".

Official policy

"If you cut off a head by mistake, there
is no way to rectify the mistake."

(Mao Zedong, "On the Ten Major Relationships,
25 April 1956)

This statement, which has often been quoted by Chinese officials, was made by Mao Zedong in 1956. However, Mao was referring only to "counter-revolutionaries in Party and government organs, schools and army units" as distinct from counter-revolutionaries "in society at large". Mao stated that those in the first category should not be executed because "such executions would yield no advantage". Unlike those in "society at large" he said they "make enemies in general but seldom enemies in particular". Therefore, Mao said, they should not be executed. This distinction between two categories of citizens prevailed for many years but has now disappeared. The new constitution adopted in 1982 states that all citizens are equal before the law (Article 33).

Although the statement by Mao is still occasionally cited by Chinese officials, since 1979 most official statements have tended to justify the increased use of the death penalty rather than caution against it. They usually explain that the death penalty is needed as an exemplary punishment and a deterrent against crime in order to "safeguard social order" and enforce the law. Many such comments on the death penalty have been made by legal and political officials in recent years. Those cited below are but a few examples.

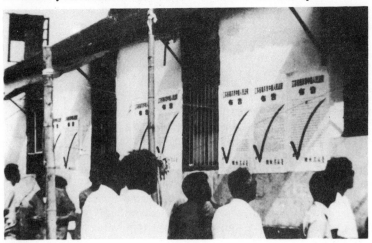

Each poster carries the details of several people who have been condemned to death: the large red tick shows that the sentences have been carried out. Nanjing, Jiangsu province, 25 September 1983.

Commenting on the punishment meted out to a group who had been convicted of "gang rape" in Hangzhou, the *Liberation Army Daily*, a Shanghai newspaper, said on 17 November 1979:

"It is an undeniably great error of judgement for some people to assume that the present time seems to be a lawless stage in which they can defy laws human and divine because the criminal law and other laws adopted by the second session of the Fifth National People's Congress will not be enforced until 1st January next year. There are imperfections in our judicial system, which needs gradual improvement; however, no one should attempt to take advantage of such imperfections. A killer must pay with his life."

(Liberation Army Daily, 17 November 1979)

On 25 February 1980, the New China News Agency cited an article published that day in the *People's Daily* which was seen by foreign correspondents in Beijing as an attempt by the government to caution local officials against using the death penalty too often, in view of the large number of executions carried out at the end of 1979.

". . . the article says: 'If we do not execute offenders who have committed the most heinous crimes, other criminal offenders will become still more unbridled in carrying out acts of violence. In that case, more innocent people will be victims of physical assault or even murder, the country's unity and stability will be sabotaged and there will be no effective guarantee for its modernization effort.'

"While in favour of capital punishment, the article points out that the country's criminal law stresses the necessity of executing as few people as possible. It quotes the law as saying: 'The death penalty shall be imposed only on offenders who have committed the most heinous crimes.' 'This is the consistent policy of our Communist Party and state', the article emphasizes. 'It doesn't matter much if execution of the convict is suspended for one or two weeks . . . but once the convict is executed, the mistake resulting from the previous wrong judgment can never be corrected', the article says."

The following statement was made by Xie Bangzhi, head of the Chinese delegation to the Sixth United Nations Congress on the Prevention of Crime and the Treatment of Offenders, Caracas, Venezuela, August-September 1980:

"Though the death penalty is still retained in China's Criminal Law, its application has been reduced to the minimum. Our Criminal Law stipulates that 'The death penalty shall be imposed only on offenders who have committed the most heinous crime.' It is spearheaded chiefly at a very small number of criminal offenders who have perpetrated crimes aimed at subverting our state power, disrupting our national construction, or gravely undermining social order by committing crimes of homicide, arson, violent robbery or rape, which cause great harm to the interests of the State or the people and which constitute flagrant criminal offences according to the law. However, China has consistently adhered to the policy of exercising strict control over the death penalty and has been firm in not executing any offender whose execution is not deemed necessary by the law."

On 12 November 1982—only nine months before the start of a wave of executions purportedly aimed at curbing the high crime rate—the *South China Morning Post*, a Hong Kong newspaper, cited a report from the official New China News Agency (NCNA) that the crime rate had fallen, and indicating that this was due to preventive measures, rather than harsh punishment:

"The NCNA reported that China's Security Forces have managed to stem the post-Mao crime wave, with offences down by nearly 16% in the first nine months of this year compared with the same period last year. It quoted a police official as saying this was because of preventive measures taken by parents, teachers and political activists against juvenile delinquency and better discipline in factories."

The first execution for embezzlement elicited the following comments in the *People's Daily* of 18 January 1983:

"This solemn warning is a heavy blow and a serious warning to the criminals who are frenziedly sabotaging our socialist economy. It will certainly give impetus to the struggle against serious criminal activities endangering socialism in economic and other fields. We are always very cautious on the question of the death sentence but we must never tolerate the tiny number of criminals who purposely sabotage the socialist system."

(*Reuters*, 19 January 1983)

The *Yangcheng Evening News*, a newspaper from Guangzhou, commented on the same case on 18 January 1983:

"Execute one as a warning to a hundred. Sometimes killing a person is worth setting off firecrackers and throwing a party to celebrate, although of course it depends on who is killed."

(*South China Morning Post*, 20 January 1983)

Following the start of the "campaign against crime" launched in

August 1983, Liu Fuzhi, Minister of Public Security, stated:

"Only by severely striking at criminal activities will it be possible for us promptly to bring about a fundamental turn for the better in maintaining social order, protect the people's democratic rights and their lives and property, strengthen the socialist legal system, . . .

"To punish severely and promptly, according to law, those criminals guilty of serious offences is of paramount importance in achieving the goal of maintaining a comprehensive social order. Particularly at a time when criminal activities are rampant, education and persuasion are hardly effective if we do not severely strike at the criminal offenders and bring into full play the role of dictatorship to frighten criminals."

(New China News Agency, 25 August 1983)

On 17 September 1983 the *South China Morning Post* reported that the *Liberation Daily*, an official newspaper from Shanghai, had acknowledged for the first time that there was concern among the population that the campaign against crime was "inhuman". However, the *Liberation Daily* reportedly said "to show magnanimity towards criminals could harm the interests of the people." A few weeks later An Zhiguo, Political Editor of the official English language weekly *Beijing Review*, wrote an editorial on capital punishment in the 7 November 1983 issue of the review, in which he referred to executions as "having occurred almost simultaneously in many parts of China". He also said:

"Meting out stern punishment, including the death penalty, to criminals, will not only give these lawbreakers what they deserve, but will also serve as a warning to other offenders and prevent further crimes . . ."

The *South China Morning Post* of 2 December 1983 quoted as follows a recent article written by a Chinese jurist, Zhang Youyu, in the official magazine *Democracy and the Legal System*:

"It is quite right to say that one should stress education in regard to young people, but those who are guilty of murder, arson, robbery and rape, especially those who are ring-leaders, must be severely dealt with. Otherwise juvenile delinquents will follow their footsteps and become criminals.

"It is regretRable that most of the criminals recently punished are young people. This could have been avoided if we had started the present campaign earlier. However, with those whose crimes are not severe, we try our best to save them through education."

Since then various official statements have been published to justify the large number of executions. Some have criticized "bourgeois humanitarians" in foreign countries who oppose the death penalty for "evil murderers".* Detailed statistics have also been published on the fall of the crime rate which, according to Chinese officials, has resulted from the stern policy towards offenders. For instance, the New China News Agency of 18 November 1983 reported on an article published that day in the official weekly *China's Legal System*:

"Criminal cases recorded an overall drop of 46.7 percent nationwide from August to September, with a 38.7 decrease in major cases. In October, there were 11.5 percent fewer criminal cases than in September, while major cases dropped a further 28.5 percent. Crime rates in September and October were the lowest in recent years, the report said.

"According to statistics from 18 major cities, the report went on, criminal cases dropped 46 percent in September, with major cases down 48 percent. Urban crime rates also continued their drop in October, it added."

Most of the statements made in recent years by Chinese officials are based on a supposition that Amnesty International believes to be incorrect: the belief that the death penalty is a more effective deterrent to certain types of crime than other punishments. In its letter to President Li Xiannian on 21 October 1983, Amnesty International stated that the death penalty cannot be justified as a fitting response to crimes, however violent or repugnant these may be. Referring to research on the effectiveness of the death penalty as a deterrent to homicide, it said:

"As far as Amnesty International is aware, however, no such studies have ever established the efficacy of the death penalty in comparison with other punishments. If no such connection has been established with regard to homicide, still less is known about the effectiveness of the death penalty as a deterrent to other crimes. It is difficult to see how the use of the death penalty as a deterrent can be justified in the absence of any evidence of this effect."

The organization also drew attention to a statement made in 1980

---

* Such criticisms were made by the *People's Daily* political commentator, Zhou Lianren, who wrote on 18 January 1984: "But if we don't punish murderers with death, and let them go off and kill more good people, is that 'humane'?" (*Reuters*, 20 January 1984)

by the United Nations Secretary General:

> "An opinion seems to prevail that the death penalty is essential to the maintenance of law and order, justifiable against singularly heinous offences, and a vital deterrent against escalation of crime. This appears to be disproved by the experience of the countries which have abolished capital punishment. It is necessary to give serious consideration to the question of capital punishment and to ways and means of its restriction since the taking of life of human beings in the name of retribution, incapacitation and an unsubstantiated deterrent effect on others clearly violates respect for the dignity of every person and the right to life as stated in the basic postulates of the United Nations."

> (Statement by Secretary-General Kurt Waldheim at the opening of the Sixth United Nations Congress on the Prevention of Crime and the Treatment of Offenders, on 25 August 1980)

Main text of a memorandum submitted by Amnesty International to the Government of the People's Republic of China

(January 1983)

I. The imprisonment of prisoners of conscience

International human rights standards provide that every person has the right freely to hold and to express his or her convictions and the obligation to extend a like freedom to others, as set out in the Universal Declaration of Human Rights, in particular in Articles 18, 19 and 20, and in the International Covenant on Civil and Political Rights, in particular in Articles 18, 19, 21 and 22*. In accordance with such standards, Amnesty International seeks to ensure the release of people who are imprisoned, detained or otherwise physically restricted by reason of their political, religious or other conscientiously held beliefs or by reason of their ethnic origin, sex, colour or language, provided they have not used or advocated violence.

In pursuance of these aims Amnesty International has appealed for the release of prisoners of conscience in the People's Republic of China over a number of years. In the past three years, it has also been concerned by a series of arrests concerning people who had merely exercised their fundamental rights to freedom of opinion, association or publication, or to freedom of religion. One group of concern to Amnesty International includes people who edited or contributed to unofficial journals. Most of these were created in late

---

* Relevant extracts of the International Covenant on Civil and Political Rights are given below:

  Article 18, paragraph 1:
  1. Everyone shall have the right to freedom of thought, conscience and religion. This right shall include freedom to have or to adopt a religion or belief of his choice, and freedom, either individually or in community with others and in public or private, to manifest his religion or belief in worship, observance, practice and teaching.

1978 in the wave of a movement calling for greater democracy in Chinese society. One of the first to have been arrested in early 1979 is Wei Jingsheng, the editor of an unofficial Beijing journal, *Exploration*. He was tried in Beijing in October 1979 and convicted of spreading "counter-revolutionary" propaganda through his writings and of passing on "military secrets" to a foreigner. Amnesty International believes that he was detained for exercising his right to freedom of expression and association and has adopted him as a prisoner of conscience. In another case, Ren Wanding and Chen Lu, both members of a group called the Chinese Human Rights Alliance, were arrested shortly after Wei Jingsheng in spring 1979. No charges have been made public against them since their arrest. They are believed to be held for exercising their right to freedom of expression.

Among others arrested later are more than 25 editors or supporters of unofficial journals who were detained in spring and summer 1981 in various provinces. Their arrest is reported to have been due in part to their attempts to organize a "National Association of Democratic Journals" and to seek official registration for their publications, as well as to their public appeals for other imprisoned editors. They include Fu Shenqi, a worker in a generator factory in Shanghai and editor of the unofficial magazine *Responsibility*; Liu Liping, a librarian in the Foundation University Library of Changsha and editor of *Bulletin of Ideals*; Qin Yongmin, a steel mill worker in Wuhan and co-founder of *The Sound of the Bell*; Xu Shuiliang, a worker in a pharmaceutical factory and university graduate from Nanjing; and others in various cities. All those arrested in spring and summer 1981 are believed to be held for their writings or publishing activities. They are not known to have used

---

Article 19, paragraphs 1 and 2:
1. Everyone shall have the right to hold opinions without interference.
2. Everyone shall have the right to freedom of expression; this right shall include freedom to seek, receive and impart information and ideas of all kinds, regardless of frontiers, either orally, in writing or in print, in the form of art, or through any other media of his choice.

Article 21:
The right of peaceful assembly shall be recognized. No restrictions may be placed on the exercise of this right other than those imposed in conformity with the law and which are necessary in a democratic society in the interests of national security or public safety, public order *(ordre public)*, the protection of public health or morals or the protection of the rights and freedom of others.

Article 22, paragraph 1:
1. Everyone shall have the right to freedom of association with others, including the right to form and join trade unions for the protection of his interests.

or advocated violence and Amnesty International has adopted them as prisoners of conscience.

Amnesty International is also concerned by the detention of 13 Roman Catholic priests and laymen from Shanghai who are reported to have been arrested in November 1981 for exercising their right to freedom of religion. In this respect, Amnesty International would like to refer to the United Nations Declaration on the Elimination of All Forms of Intolerance and of Discrimination Based on Religion or Belief, which was adopted by the United Nations General Assembly without a vote on 25 November 1981. The Declaration states that the right to freedom of religion or belief includes the following freedoms:

(a) To worship or assemble in connection with a religion or belief, and to establish and maintain places for these purposes;

(b) To establish and maintain appropriate charitable or humanitarian institutions;

(c) To make, acquire and use to an adequate extent the necessary articles and materials related to the rites or customs of a religion or belief;

(d) To write, issue and disseminate relevant publications in these areas;

(e) To teach a religion or belief in places suitable for these purposes;

(f) To solicit and receive voluntary financial and other contributions from individuals and institutions;

(g) To train, appoint, elect or designate by succession appropriate leaders called for by the requirements and standards of any religion or belief;

(h) To observe days of rest and to celebrate holidays and ceremonies in accordance with the precepts of one's religion or belief;

(i) To establish and maintain communications with individuals and communities in matters of religion and belief at the national and international levels.

(Article VI)

To Amnesty International's knowledge, none of the priests and lay Catholics arrested in Shanghai in November 1981 had done more than exercise peacefully some of the rights enumerated above. Most of them are priests in their sixties or seventies who had already spent on average 20 years in detention, having been first arrested in the mid-1950s for refusing to cooperate with the official Patriotic Catholic Association. One of them, Zhu Hongsheng, now aged 67, was first arrested in 1955 together with the Bishop of Shanghai,

Gong Pinmei, who is still currently detained in Shanghai after 28 years in prison. Father Zhu Hongsheng was tried together with others in 1960 and sentenced to 15 years' imprisonment. He was released in 1979 and returned to Shanghai where he stayed until his rearrest in November 1981. No official information has been made public about the charges and whereabouts of Father Zhu Hongsheng or the other priests and lay Catholics detained. However, Zhu Hongsheng is reported to have been charged with: 1) participating in an unauthorized pilgrimage to Zose (a shrine to the Virgin Mary on the outskirts of Shanghai); 2) communicating Vatican directives to Catholics in China; and 3) sending religious information about China abroad.

Other cases of people detained for their religious beliefs have been reported by private sources to Amnesty International, such as that of Karma Dhorong, a 44-year-old Tibetan hermit of Jodha district in the Autonomous Region of Tibet, who is reported to have been arrested in December 1980 in Lhasa for preaching Buddhism, and that of Nyazak Gotulku, a Tibetan Lama, arrested in early 1980 in the village of Rongpatsa, near Kanze, on suspicion of being the author of a prophecy which he reportedly denied having written. He is reported to have been held since then in a labour camp at Myniak.

With regard to some of the cases mentioned above, Amnesty International would like to submit some remarks regarding certain provisions of Chinese legislation under which people are detained for the non-violent exercise of their fundamental human rights.

a) The Criminal Law

Amnesty International is concerned that several articles of the Criminal Law have been used to imprison people who had merely exercised peacefully their fundamental rights. It is particularly concerned about Articles 98 and 102 which stipulate that:

"Those organizing or leading a counter-revolutionary group will be sentenced to fixed-term imprisonment of not less than five years. Those taking an active part will be sentenced to fixed-term imprisonment, detention, surveillance or deprivation of political rights for not more than five years."

(Article 98)

"Any of the following acts carried out for counter-revolutionary purposes will be punishable by fixed-term imprisonment, detention, surveillance or deprivation of political rights for not less than five years:

1) inciting the masses to resist arrest and violating the law and statute of the State;

2) using counter-revolutionary slogans, leaflets or other means to spread propaganda inciting the overthrow of the political power of the dictatorship of the proletariat and the socialist system.''

(Article 102)

Amnesty International has noted that other articles of the section on ''counter-revolutionary'' offences in the Criminal Law deal specifically with political offences involving violence or acts endangering the security of the state, such as hijacking, espionage, incitement to defection in the armed forces, etc. It is concerned, however, that Articles 98 and 102 do not appear to refer specifically to acts of violence, but rather to the right to freedom of opinion, association and to dissemination of information. The use of slogans, leaflets or peaceful assembly to circulate opinions or beliefs is in itself a peaceful activity. It should not be treated as a criminal offence whatever the beliefs or opinions expressed provided that these do not advocate violence. The general definition of ''counter-revolutionary'' offences given in Article 90 of the Criminal Law does not indicate whether such offences refer specifically to acts of violence or to the advocacy of violent acts. Article 90 reads:

''Counter-revolutionary offences are those for the purpose of overthrowing the political power of the dictatorship of the proletariat and the socialist system and jeopardizing the People's Republic of China.''

The law gives no further clarification of what may constitute ''incitement to overthrow the dictatorship of the proletariat or socialist system''. It may therefore be subject to varying interpretations and result in giving those in charge of enforcing the law the power to sentence people for their opinions or beliefs rather than violent acts.

Amnesty International has been disturbed at recent reports that Wang Xizhe and He Qiu, two young men from Guangzhou adopted by Amnesty International as prisoners of conscience, were tried and convicted of ''counter-revolutionary'' offences under these provisions. Wang Xizhe is reported to have been convicted under Articles 98 and 102 of the Criminal Law and sentenced to 14 years' imprisonment and deprivation of political rights for an additional four and a half years at his trial on 28 May 1982 in Guangzhou. He Qiu is reported to have been sentenced to 10 years' imprisonment under Article 98 of the criminal law on 29 May 1982. Before their arrests, they had edited or contributed to unofficial journals and joined in appeals for the release of other imprisoned editors*. These are believed to be the reasons for their conviction. No details of their trial have been officially made public.

These provisions of the Criminal Law are also reported to have been used recently in another case—that of Xu Wenli, a worker and former editor of the unofficial journal *April Fifth Tribune*, who was arrested in Beijing in April 1981. No official information about his reported trial has been made public. However, according to a document alleged to be the record of the court judgment in his case, published in the Hong Kong review *Baixing* on 16 October 1982, Xu Wenli was tried on 8 June 1982 by Beijing Intermediate People's Court and sentenced to 15 years' imprisonment and four years' deprivation of political rights on charges of "organizing a counter-revolutionary clique" and "counter-revolutionary propaganda and agitation". This document states that Xu Wenli's conviction and sentence was based on the provisions of Articles 90, 98, 102, 52, 51 (1), 64 and 60** of the Criminal Law of the People's Republic of China. It details the specific accusations brought against him and others reported to have been involved in his alleged "counter-revolutionary group". These accusations include: forming, in June 1980, a "Chinese Communist Alliance" with the alleged aim of "destroying the dictatorship of one party" and planning the publication of a "Study Bulletin" and the creation of a "Chinese Association for the Promotion of Democratic Unity" with an office in Hong Kong. It also refers to Xu Wenli's writings and protests against some official measures and to the dissemination of his writings abroad as being "counter-revolutionary propaganda and agitation". None of the accusations detailed in this document, whether or not they are founded, indicate that Xu Wenli or others alleged to have been associated with him had used or advocated violence.

---

* Wang Xizhe, in particular, is reported to have written an "Open Letter to the National People's Congress concerning the arrest of Liu Qing", an editor of the *April Fifth Tribune*, after the latter was detained on 11 November 1979 in Beijing for selling the transcript of the trial of Wei Jingsheng. Wang Xizhe had been detained on several occasions previously. In 1974, together with several others, he wrote and displayed in Guangzhou a long wall-poster entitled "On Socialist Democracy and the Legal System" and signed Li Yizhe. As a result, Wang Xizhe and the co-authors of the poster spent several years in prison. Though the poster primarily criticized the policies followed by Lin Biao and the "Gang of Four" (who were arrested in 1976), Wang Xizhe and the others were not released and rehabilitated until January 1979.

** Articles 52 and 51 (1) refer to the deprivation of political rights, Article 64 to punishment for several crimes at the same time and Article 60 to confiscation of personal belongings.

b) The law on "re-education through labour"

Another law under which prisoners of conscience are detained is the 1957 Decision of the State Council of the People's Republic of China on the Question of Re-education Through Labour. It provides for the detention without trial of people considered to have "anti-socialist views" or to be "hooligans", for the stated purpose of "re-educating them through labour". The law further states that it applies to people whose crimes are considered too minor for them to be charged with an offence and brought to trial. It provides that those concerned can be assigned to carry out "re-education through labour" on simple decision by the police, without being charged or tried. According to supplementary regulations adopted in November 1979, the length of such "re-education" is from one to three years and this can be further extended by a maximum of one year.

Amnesty International is concerned that this law institutes detention without charge or trial for people held on political grounds. As they are not charged, they cannot question the grounds for their detention or appeal against it before a court of law. This law thus deprives some citizens of the People's Republic of China of the rights and protections to which they are entitled according to the constitution and other current laws of the People's Republic of China. It is also at variance with the international standards against arbitrary detention, as laid down for example in Article 9 of the International Covenant on Civil and Political Rights, of which relevant parts read:

"Everyone has the right to liberty and security of person.
No one shall be subjected to arbitrary arrest or detention.
No one shall be deprived of his liberty except on such
grounds and in accordance with such procedure as are
established by law."

(Article 9, 1)

"Anyone who is arrested shall be informed, at the time of
arrest, of the reasons for his arrest and shall be promptly
informed of any charges against him."

(Article 9, 2)

"Anyone who is deprived of his liberty by arrest or
detention shall be entitled to take proceedings before a
court, in order that the court may decide without delay on
the lawfulness of his detention and order his release if the
detention is not lawful."

(Article 9, 4)

Several cases of prisoners of conscience detained without trial for "re-education through labour" have been adopted by Amnesty International. One of them is Liu Qing (real name Liu Jianwei), a 35-year-old technician and joint editor of the unofficial journal *April Fifth Forum*. Liu Qing was arrested on 11 November 1979 in Beijing in connection with the sale of the unofficial transcript of a political trial. He subsequently spent several months in detention without being charged or told the exact reasons for his detention. In mid-1980, he was assigned to carry out three years of "re-education through labour" in a labour camp. His family was then reportedly informed that this was based on three grounds: (1) taking part in a demonstration by peasants in Beijing in January 1979, (2) participating in the sale of the transcript of Wei Jingsheng's trial, and (3) stealing and making out false sickness certificates—an allegation which according to Liu Qing's relations was unfounded. Liu Qing was sent to the "Temple of the Lotus Flower" labour camp in Shaanxi province. According to a testimony* which he addressed to the Chinese authorities in January 1981, the camp is surrounded by high walls topped by electrified wire and guarded by armed soldiers and police dogs. Both convicted prisoners and people undergoing "re-education through labour" are subjected to hard labour, consisting of transporting heavy stones. Liu Qing was due to be released in November 1982. However, according to reports, he was brought to trial in Beijing in August 1982 and sentenced to seven years' imprisonment. No official statement or information has been made public about Liu Qing's trial and the charges against him are unknown.

(The names of other prisoners of conscience reported to have been assigned to "re-education through labour" were included in a list in an appendix submitted to the government.)

II. Protections against arbitrary detention and prolonged detention without trial

Amnesty International opposes the arbitrary detention or prolonged detention without trial of any political prisoners and seeks the observance of the relevant standards laid down in the International Covenant on Civil and Political Rights with respect to such prisoners. Relevant extracts of the Covenant read:

"Everyone has the right to liberty and security of person.

---

* This testimony was hand-written and has been authenticated by friends of Liu Qing as being in his hand-writing.

No one shall be subjected to arbitrary arrest or detention. No one shall be deprived of his liberty except on such grounds and in accordance with such procedure as are established by law."

(Article 9, 1)

"Anyone arrested or detained on a criminal charge shall be brought promptly before a judge or other officer authorized by law to exercise judicial power and shall be entitled to trial within a reasonable time or to release. It shall not be the general rule that persons awaiting trial shall be detained in custody, but release may be subject to guarantees to appear for trial, at any other stage of the judicial proceedings, and, should occasion arise, for execution of the judgement."

(Article 9, 3)

a) Arbitrary detention

With regard to protection against arbitrary detention, Amnesty International has noted that the Arrest and Detention Act of the People's Republic of China, adopted in February 1979, and the Law of Criminal Procedure, which came into force in January 1980, afford protections to PRC citizens against arbitrary arrest or detention. Article 44 of the Law of Criminal Procedure provides that "interrogation of a detainee shall be performed within 24 hours by the detaining public security organs. Where it is found that no grounds for arrest exist, the detainee shall be released immediately and given a release certificate." Article 43 of this law also states that within 24 hours after a person is arrested, the family of the detainee (or the unit where he/she works) shall be informed of the reasons for detention and the place of detention. Furthermore, three days after a person is detained (or maximum seven days in "special cases"), the police (public security) must submit the case to a people's procuratorate for approval and the latter must decide on whether or not to sanction the arrest within three days (Article 48 of the Criminal Procedure Law). Thus, within seven days after initial detention (maximum 10 days in "special cases"), a person should be either formally arrested with the sanction of a people's procuratorate or released.

Article 143 of the Criminal Law also prohibits unlawful detention in these terms:

"It is strictly forbidden to incarcerate a person unlawfully or to deprive him of personal freedom unlawfully by other means. Anyone who violates this will be sentenced to detention, deprivation of political rights or imprisonment for not more than three years. If beatings or insults are involved, the offender will be severely punished.

"Whoever commits the aforesaid offence and causes severe injury to another person will be sentenced to imprisonment for not less than three years and not more than 10; if he causes death to another person, he will be sentenced to imprisonment for not less than seven years."

Article 41 of the new constitution provides for the right to make complaints against any state organ or functionary transgressing the law and prohibits suppression of such appeals or retaliation against those making them.

Amnesty International has welcomed the introduction of these provisions in Chinese legislation. It is concerned, however, by reports indicating that these protections against arbitrary detention are often inoperative in practice and that people have been detained for long periods without being charged or told the reasons for their detention. One example is the case of Liu Qing, which was mentioned earlier (page 90). According to reports published abroad, he reported in a testimony being held for several months after his arrest without being told the precise reasons for his detention. Throughout that period, his family was reportedly not able to visit him or exchange correspondence with him, nor were they informed of the reason for his arrest. According to his testimony, he addressed two letters to the authorities to protest against his illegal detention. He reports giving the first letter on 21 January 1980 to a prison guard who promised to transmit it to Beijing People's Procuratorate and the second one to another guard on 5 April 1980. The second letter was addressed to the Supreme People's Court and Supreme People's Procuratorate. In his letters, Liu Qing accused Beijing Public Security Bureau of detaining him illegally and using forced confessions. He neither received a reply nor an acknowledgement to either letter.

Other reports from private sources allege that it is common practice for people accused or suspected of political offences to be held incommunicado for long periods without being told the precise reasons for their detention or their family informed of their place of detention or the reason for their arrest. In the light of such reports, Amnesty International believes that there is a need to introduce procedures whereby the family, friends or legal representative of a person detained could call upon an independent judicial authority within 24 hours after that person has been placed in custody in order to be informed of the reasons for detention and place of detention. This might help to ensure the effective application of Article 43 of the Law of Criminal Procedure and other relevant provisions and would be in line with Resolution 34/178 adopted on 17 December 1979 by the United Nations General Assembly on "The Right of *Amparo*, *Habeas Corpus* or other Legal Remedies to the Same Effect", of which relevant extracts read:

"The General Assembly, . . .

1. Expresses its conviction that the application within the legal system of States of *amparo*, *habeas corpus* or other legal remedies to the same effect is of fundamental importance for:

(a) Protecting persons against arbitrary arrest and unlawful detention;

(b) Effecting the release of persons who are detained by reason of their political opinions or convictions, including in pursuance of trade union activities;

(c) Clarifying the whereabouts and fate of missing and disappeared persons;

2. Considers that the use of these remedies may also forestall opportunities for persons exercising power over detainees to engage in torture or other cruel, inhuman or degrading treatment or punishment.

3. Calls upon all Governments to guarantee to persons within their jurisdiction the full enjoyment of the right of *amparo*, *habeas corpus* or other legal remedies to the same effect, as may be applicable in their legal system;

. . .".

b) Prolonged detention without trial

With regard to protections against prolonged detention without trial, Amnesty International has noted that paragraph 1 of Article 92 of the Law of Criminal Procedure fixes at two or three months the maximum period of time (after formal arrest) before a decision is taken on whether or not to start prosecution against a detainee. Paragraph 1 reads as follows:

"The maximum period for an accused to be detained pending preliminary investigations shall not exceed two months. If the circumstances of a case are complicated and the investigation of the case is not concluded after two months, an extension of one month may be granted by the People's Procuratorate at the next level."

However, Amnesty International has noted with concern the provision of paragraph 2 of the same article which provides that if a case is "particularly serious and complicated" and the investigation is not concluded within a maximum of three months, an unspecified time extension can be granted by the Standing Committee of the National People's Congress. These provisions permit indefinite detention without trial in contravention to all the other protections afforded by the Criminal Procedure Law. They also deviate from the principles enunciated in Article 9 of the International Covenant on Civil and Political Rights which was cited earlier.

Amnesty International is concerned that these provisions may have been used in the cases of a number of prisoners of conscience arrested in the past three years. According to two student union leaders from Hong Kong, who visited the People's Republic of China in early May 1982 to inquire about the fate of the editors of unofficial journals detained since spring 1981, officials from the Chief Public Prosecutor's Office and Beijing Public Security Bureau stated that some of those arrested had been held for long periods without trial after permission had been obtained from the National People's Congress Standing Committee "as required by law". This would seem to confirm that the provisions of Article 92 (paragraph 2) of the Law of Criminal Procedure have been applied in at least some cases.

Illustrative of the cases of prisoners detained for long periods without trial known to Amnesty International are those of Ren Wanding and Chen Lu, whose cases were mentioned earlier (page 84). Both of them have been adopted by Amnesty International as prisoners of conscience. Ren Wanding was arrested on 4 April 1979 in Beijing while pasting up a poster on the "democracy wall". Chen Lu was arrested on 29 March 1979 in Beijing. Neither of them are known to have been tried. No charges were ever made public against them. Their whereabouts have been unknown since 1979. They have now been held for more than three years without any news of them having reached their friends since their arrest. Their continued arbitrary detention after three years appears to be in clear contravention of international human rights standards.

III. Trial procedures

In accordance with its mandate, Amnesty International seeks to ensure that any trial procedures relating to political prisoners should conform to internationally established norms, such as those stipulated in Articles 14 and 15 of the International Covenant on Civil and Political Rights. Article 14 of the Covenant provides that:

> "1) All persons shall be equal before the courts and tribunals. In the determination of any criminal charge against him, or of his rights and obligations in a suit at law, everyone shall be entitled to a fair and public hearing by a competent, independent and impartial tribunal established by law. (. . .)
>
> 2) Everyone charged with a criminal offence shall have the right to be presumed innocent until proven guilty according to law.
>
> 3) In the determination of any criminal charge against him, everyone shall be entitled to the following minimum guarantees, in full equality:
>
> (a) To be informed promptly and in detail in a language which he understands of the nature and cause of the charge against him;
>
> (b) To have adequate time and facilities for the preparation of his defence and to communicate with counsel of his own choosing;
>
> (c) To be tried without undue delay;
>
> (d) To be tried in his presence, and to defend himself in person or through legal assistance of his own choosing; to be informed, if he does not have legal assistance, of this right; and to have legal assistance assigned to him, in any case where the interests of justice so require, and without payment by him in any such case if he does not have sufficient means to pay for it;
>
> (e) To examine, or have examined, the witnesses against him and to obtain the attendance and examination of witnesses on his behalf under the same conditions as witnesses against him;
>
> (f) To have the free assistance of an interpreter if he cannot understand or speak the language used in court;
>
> (g) Not to be compelled to testify against himself or to confess guilt.
>
> (. . .)"

On several occasions in the past, Amnesty International has expressed concern to the authorities of the People's Republic of China about the conditions under which political prisoners were tried, particularly with reference to the principles that everyone is entitled to a public hearing by an independent and impartial tribunal and that an accused shall be presumed innocent until proven guilty according to law.

When the Law of Criminal Procedure came into force in January 1980, Amnesty International noted with interest the provisions of Article 111 according to which all cases should be heard in public, except those involving state secrets or personal secrets. It also welcomed the provisions of Article 110 (paragraph 5), which state that if a case is to be heard in public, the main points of the case, name of the accused and time and place of the opening court session should be announced in advance. To Amnesty International's knowledge, however, no such public announcements were made in a number of recent trials of political prisoners. In several cases which have come to the organization's attention, the trials are reported to have been either closed to the public or open only to a selected audience from which friends of the defendants were usually excluded.

Among such cases are those of Wang Xizhe and He Qiu, two editors of unofficial journals from Guangzhou (see above, page 87). They are reported to have been tried at the end of May 1982 and sentenced respectively to 14 and 10 years' imprisonment for "counter-revolutionary" offences. To date, no official information or statement about the trials has been made public, though according to private sources, officials from Guangzhou acknowledged that the trials had taken place and stated that the defendants had been provided with lawyers. According to the same sources, the families of the defendants were not notified in advance about the trials and He Qiu's wife only heard about her husband's trial when it was already under way. By the time she reached the court, the trial was over.

Amnesty International was also concerned by reports regarding the trial in June 1982 in Beijing of Xu Wenli, whose case was mentioned earlier (page 88). As in the case of Wang Xizhe and He Qiu, no official announcement or information about the trial has been made public, contrary to the provisions of Articles 111 and 110 of the Law of Criminal Procedure, and, as far as is known, the trial was not held openly. According to a document said to be the court judgment on Xu Wenli's case, others who are named had apparently been charged in connection with Xu's case and were to be brought to trial separately. As of January 1983, however, the status of their cases remains unknown.

Another prisoner of conscience adopted by Amnesty International, Liu Qing, was also reported recently to have been tried secretly in

Beijing (see above, page 90). No official information has been made public about the trial and the specific charges brought against him are not known. He is said to have been sentenced to seven years' imprisonment after being tried in Beijing in August 1982 for "counter-revolutionary" offences. His brother Liu Nianchun, and another editor of an unofficial journal, Lu Lin, are also reported to have been brought to trial in Beijing at the same time but no details are known about their cases.

The absence of hearings open to the general public has also been reported in the cases of several former student leaders of the Cultural Revolution whose trial is said to have started in Beijing in late October 1982. They include Kuai Dafu, former leader of the "Earth Rebel" faction at Qinghua University in Beijing, Nie Yuanzi, a lecturer in the philosophy department of Beijing University who became famous for writing in 1966 a big-character poster exhorting the students to revolt, and others reported to have been detained since 1978. News of their trial was published on 4 November 1982 in the Hong Kong newspaper *Ta Kong Pao* and subsequently reported by foreign correspondents in Beijing. According to these reports, the trial was conducted in closed session with a selected audience; the total number of defendants involved and the precise charges against them was unknown. As of January 1983, no further information has become available whether from official or other sources about this trial.

Amnesty International has noted the provisions of Article 26 of the Law of Criminal Procedure which allows the defendant to entrust a lawyer (or other citizens permitted by a People's Court) to "prepare" his defence. However, it has also noted with concern that the law includes no provisions to ensure that a defendant be presumed innocent until proven guilty. According to information it has received, lawyers appointed for the defence of political prisoners usually only plead mitigation rather than contesting the validity of the charges themselves. In none of the cases of political prisoners which have come to Amnesty International's attention over the past three years has there been any indication that witnesses have been called to testify in court for the defence. In some cases, such as that of Wei Jingsheng who was tried in Beijing in October 1979 (see page 84), reports in the official press clearly indicated that there was an official assumption of the defendant's guilt at the onset of the trial. They referred to him as a "counter-revolutionary" while the trial was still on, thus prejudicing its outcome. Furthermore, the official press reports on the trial dealt mainly with the prosecution case against Wei Jingsheng and did not include any information on a statement by him in his own defence.

In this respect, Amnesty International is also concerned by the lack of transcripts or detailed public records on a number of trials of political prisoners reported to have been held in the past five years. Among the cases of concern to Amnesty International are those of three printing workers from Taiyuan (Shanxi Province), Chen Yuming, Zhang Jiaxin and Wang Jianwei. All the information publicly available on their cases appears to be based on a report in the *Taiyuan Daily* of 27 February 1981. According to this report they had been tried some time previously in Taiyuan and sentenced to short terms of imprisonment, for forming in 1979 their own political party and demanding a "government of union" in China. As far as is known to Amnesty International, no other details were made public about the case and circumstances of the trial, and the requests for information addressed to the Chinese authorities by Amnesty International groups since 1981 have not been answered.

Another example is the case of Guo Shuzhang, who according to a brief report by Zhengzhou radio on 18 December 1979 was tried in Xinxiang (Henan Province) on 9 December 1979 during a "rally" organized by the "political and legal organs" of the city. He was further reported to have been sentenced to eight years' imprisonment by Xinxiang Intermediate People's Court on charges of having "sent counter-revolutionary letters" and "put up counter-revolutionary posters" on the front doors of the offices of the local Party Committee in Xinxiang on 25 October 1979. According to the official report, his letters and posters were appealing in favour of Wei Jingsheng who had been tried in Beijing earlier that month. To Amnesty International's knowledge, no further official information was made public about the case and Amnesty International groups have not received any replies from the Chinese authorities to their requests for information about it.

Several aspects of Guo Shuzhang's case are of concern to Amnesty International, including the reference in the report mentioned above that his trial took place during a "rally". According to information available to Amnesty International, such rallies or "mass trials" usually involve large numbers of participants and do not provide the opportunity for the accused to defend themselves against the accusations.

IV. Reported ill-treatment of prisoners and conditions of detention

Amnesty International opposes by all appropriate means the infliction of torture or other cruel, inhuman or degrading treatment or punishment on prisoners or other detained or restricted persons whether or not they have used or advocated violence. In this work, Amnesty International bases itself on the standards laid down in the International Covenant on Civil and Political Rights and other more specific instruments such as the UN Standard Minimum Rules for the Treatment of Prisoners, adopted by the UN Economic and Social Council in 1957, the Code of Conduct for Law Enforcement Officials, adopted by the UN General Assembly on 17 December 1979, and the Declaration on the Protection of All Persons from Torture and Other Cruel, Inhuman or Degrading Treatment or Punishment, adopted by the UN General Assembly on 9 December 1975. Articles 3 and 9 of this declaration read:

> "No State may permit or tolerate torture or other cruel, inhuman or degrading treatment or punishment. Exceptional circumstances such as a state of war or a threat of war, internal political instability or any other public emergency may not be invoked as a justification of torture or other cruel, inhuman or degrading treatment or punishment."
>
> *(Article 3)*

> "Wherever there is a reasonable ground to believe that an act of torture as defined in article 1 has been committed, the competent authorities of the State concerned shall promptly proceed to an impartial investigation even if there has been no formal complaint."
>
> *(Article 9)*

Amnesty International has noted and welcomed the provisions of Article 32 of the Law of Criminal Procedure of the People's Republic of China which states that "to extract confessions by torture or under duress, or to collect evidence by means of threats, enticement, deceit or other illegal means" is strictly forbidden. It has also noted that Article 136 of the Criminal Law provides for the punishment of state functionaries who extract a confession by torture.

In its report *Political Imprisonment in the People's Republic of China*, published in 1978, Amnesty International expressed concern at the frequent use of shackles, solitary confinement and "struggle sessions" either to punish convicted prisoners or to put pressure on untried prisoners to confess to "crimes". According to more recent reports, such practices still exist and prisoners have been subjected to other forms of ill-treatment, particularly before trial, while in detention centres administered by public security officers. According to former detainees, beatings are common in detention centres. Liu Qing, whose case was mentioned earlier (see page 90), reports having been beaten and forced to wear a gas mask, as well as being held in solitary confinement in a cold and wet cell for several months after his arrest in November 1979, to the extent that he started losing his hair and his eyesight was affected. According to him and other sources, Zhang Wenhe, a former member of the Chinese Human Rights Alliance who in 1980 was also held at the Detention Centre of Beijing Prison No. 1, was forced to wear hand-shackles with his hands tied behind his back, continuously for several months. He was also reportedly ill-treated in other ways. As a result his mental health is said to have been affected and he was reported to have been transferred to the Anding mental hospital in Beijing in 1981. His present circumstances and conditions are unknown.

Among other cases of concern to Amnesty International is that of Wei Jingsheng who is reported to have been held in solitary confinement incommunicado since his trial in October 1979 and to be held in the section of Beijing Prison No. 1 reserved for people sentenced to death. This would appear to be contrary to a circular reported to have been issued in 1979 by the Minister of Public Security, Zhao Cangbi, prohibiting the detention of prisoners for long periods in isolation cells on humanitarian grounds.

Amnesty International is aware that difficulties in the application of the law may occur due to misperception or abuse by individual police officers. It is also aware of cases where public security officers have been prosecuted in the People's Republic of China for ill-treating detainees. It is concerned, however, that the law affords little protection against ill-treatment apart from the stipulation that torture to extract a confession is prohibited—which, in itself, does not constitute a sufficient safeguard. In Amnesty International's experience only specific safeguards can help to prevent abuses. Such safeguards should include in particular the right for the prisoners to receive mail and visits from their families, friends and lawyers shortly after arrest and regularly thereafter. The UN Standard Minimum Rules for the Treatment of Prisoners provides in this respect:

> "An untried prisoner shall be allowed to inform immediately his family of his detention and shall be given all reasonable facilities for communicating with his family and friends, and for receiving visits from them, subject only to such restrictions and supervisions as are necessary in the interests of the administration of justice and of the security and good order of the institution."
>
> *(Article 92)*

Also of particular relevance are the safeguards recommended by the Human Rights Committee set up under the International Covenant on Civil and Political Rights in one of the "General Comments" on Article 7 of the Covenant which it adopted at its sixteenth session in Geneva in July 1982:

> "Most States have penal provisions which are applicable to cases of torture or similar practices. Because such cases nevertheless occur, it follows (. . .) that States must ensure an effective protection through some machinery of control. Complaints about ill-treatment must be investigated effectively by competent authorities. Those found guilty must be held responsible, and the alleged victims must themselves have effective remedies at their disposal, including the right to obtain compensation. Among the safeguards which may make control effective are provisions against detention incommunicado, granting, without prejudice to the investigation, persons such as doctors, lawyers and family members access to the detainees; provisions requiring that detainees should be held in places that are publicly recognised and that their names and places of detention should be entered in a central register available to persons concerned, such as relatives; provisions making confessions or other evidence obtained through torture or other treatment contrary to article 7 inadmissible in court; and measures of training and instruction of law enforcement officials not to apply such treatment."
>
> GENERAL COMMENT 7(16)*b*/(article 7)
> (UN Doc. CCPR/C/21/Add 1 of 26 August 1982)

V. The death penalty

Amnesty International works towards the abolition of the death penalty and opposes the imposition of death sentences in all cases without reservation. This is based on the belief that every human being has the inherent right to life and the right not to be subjected to torture or cruel, inhuman or degrading treatment or punishment.

Over the years, Amnesty International has sent appeals to the authorities of the People's Republic of China for the commutation of death sentences. It has been concerned by the extensive use of the death penalty and has noted that the laws of the People's Republic of China provide for the death penalty as a punishment for a number of political and criminal offences.

Since 1981, the People's Republic of China has broadened the range of offences punishable by the death penalty and adopted legislation which resulted in a marked increase in the number of executions. In communications with the Chairman of the National People's Congress (NPC) of the People's Republic of China in July and September 1981, Amnesty International expressed concern at the number of death sentences and executions reported to have taken place following the adoption on 10 June 1981 of a decree according to which, for a period of three years, the Supreme People's Court would no longer be required to review automatically all death sentences imposed by lower courts for offences such as murder, robbery, rape, arson and sabotage, though the approval of the Supreme People's Court would still be required for embezzlement and "counter-revolutionary" offences. The stated aim of the authorities in adopting this measure was to reduce the backlog of cases awaiting judgment by the Supreme People's Court. At the same time, the NPC Standing Committee also adopted the "Provisional Regulations of the People's Republic of China on Punishing Servicemen who Commit Offences Against Their Duties" which provide for the death penalty as an alternative punishment for 10 categories of serious offences. Some of these, such as "providing military secrets to enemies or foreigners" apply not only to military personnel, but also to civilians whether in time of peace or war. Since the adoption of these measures, the NPC has also adopted an amendment to the Criminal Law which further broadens the range of offences punishable by the death penalty. The amendment, which came into force on 1 April 1982, provides heavier punishments, including the death penalty, for economic crimes such as smuggling, bribery, drug-trafficking and currency offences.

The adoption of these measures is contrary to the spirit of several UN declarations and resolutions which reaffirm the desirability of restricting the number of offences punishable by the death penalty with a view to its eventual abolition. In one of the "General Comments" on Article 6 of the International Covenant on Civil and Political Rights adopted by the Human Rights Committee set up under the Covenant at its sixteenth session in Geneva in July 1982, the Committee stated:

> "While it follows from article 6(2) to (6) that States parties are not obliged to abolish the death penalty totally, they are obliged to limit its use and, in particular, to abolish it for other than the 'most serious crimes'. (. . .) The article also refers generally to abolition in terms which strongly suggest (paras. 2(2) and (6)) that abolition is desirable. The Committee concludes that all measures of abolition should

be considered as progress in the enjoyment of the right to life within the meaning of article 40, and should as such be reported to the Committee. The Committee notes that a number of States have already abolished the death penalty or suspended its application. Nevertheless, States' reports show that progress made towards abolishing or limiting the application of the death penalty is quite inadequate.

"The Committee is of the opinion that the expression 'most serious crimes' must be read restrictively to mean that the death penalty should be a quite exceptional measure. It also follows from the express terms of article 6 that it can only be imposed in accordance with the law in force at the time of the commission of the crime and not contrary to the Covenant. The procedural guarantees therein prescribed must be observed, including the right to a fair hearing by an independent tribunal, the presumption of innocence, the minimum guarantees for the defence, and the right to review by a higher tribunal. These rights are applicable in addition to the particular right to seek pardon or commutation of the sentence."

GENERAL COMMENT 6(16)*b*/(article 6)
(UN Doc. CCPR/C/21/Add 1 of 26 August 1982)

Amnesty International is aware that some death sentences in the People's Republic of China are pronounced with a two-year reprieve. However, whereas wide publicity is given by the Chinese authorities to the announcement of death sentences, there is no public reporting on what happens when the period of reprieve ends for people who have been sentenced to death with suspension of execution for two years. Since January 1981, Amnesty International groups have sent appeals to the Chinese authorities about cases of people under a suspended death sentence. However, no information has been provided or published by the Chinese authorities as to whether these death sentences have been commuted.

Conclusions and recommendations

Amnesty International has welcomed the steps taken by the government of the People's Republic of China (PRC) during recent years to restore the rule of law and towards ensuring that regular legal processes are re-established, particularly with the adoption of the Criminal Law and the Law of Criminal Procedure which came into effect in January 1980. Amnesty International is mindful of the significance of the adoption of this legislation after years when legal processes were generally ignored following the upheavals of the Cultural Revolution. It hopes that the progress made will soon enable the PRC to ratify the International Covenant on Civil and Political Rights and its Optional Protocol.

Amnesty International has also noted with interest the new constitution which was adopted on 4 December 1982 by the Fifth National People's Congress of the PRC. It welcomes those provisions of the new constitution which guarantee a number of fundamental human rights, particularly in Article 35*, and in Articles 37, 38 and 39, under which the freedom of person, the personal dignity and the homes of citizens are declared inviolable. However, it has noted with concern that the new constitution no longer guarantees some fundamental rights which were included in the 1978 constitution—such as freedom of correspondence, freedom of publication and the freedom to strike—and that it contains provisions which restrict the freedoms it proclaims. For instance, whereas Article 35 guarantees freedom of speech, the press and demonstration, Article 1, paragraph 2, invites limitation of these rights by stating:

> "The socialist system is the fundamental system of the PRC. Any person is prohibited from using any means whatsoever to undermine the socialist system."

Equally, while Article 36 guarantees "freedom of religious beliefs", it also contains provisions which may be interpreted to limit this right by providing that "no one may make use of religion to engage in activities that disrupt public order, impair the health of citizens or interfere with the educational system of the state. Religious bodies and religious affairs are not subject to any foreign domination". Amnesty International would like to refer in this respect to the relevant extracts of the Declaration of the Elimination of All Forms of Intolerance and of Discrimination Based on Religion or Belief (adopted by the United Nations General Assembly on 25 November 1981) which were cited earlier (see page 0).

With reference to official statements indicating that continuous work is being done to amend and improve the constitution and laws of the PRC, Amnesty International would like to suggest that the provisions of the constitution mentioned above be revised in line with international human rights standards so as to prevent the imprisonment of prisoners of conscience. It would also like to make the following recommendations concerning those aspects of Chinese law and legal practice of concern to Amnesty International which

---

* Article 35 reads: "Citizens of the PRC enjoy freedom of speech, of the press, of assembly, of association, of procession and of demonstration."

were described in detail in the preceding sections.

Amnesty International respectfully urges the government of the People's Republic of China to release all persons who are imprisoned, detained or otherwise physically restricted by reasons of their political, religious or other conscientiously held beliefs or by reason of their ethnic origin, sex, colour or language, who have not used or advocated violence. The cases of several such prisoners of conscience are mentioned in detail in this memorandum.

Amnesty International respectfully recommends that the government considers revising the provisions of the criminal law which permits the imprisonment of people solely for the peaceful exercise of fundamental rights, particularly Articles 98 and 102. It also urges the government to repeal the provisions of the 1957 Decision of the State Council on the Question of Rehabilitation Through Labour under which people having dissenting views can be detained without charge or trial and subjected to compulsory labour for the purposes of "re-education through labour".

With regard to the prolonged detention without trial of people held on political grounds, Amnesty International respectfully recommends that the government considers modifying the provisions of Article 92 (2) of the Law of Criminal Procedure so as to establish safeguards against unlimited detention without trial. It further recommends that consideration be given to the adoption of specific safeguards against arbitrary detention, such as procedures whereby the family, friends or legal representative of a person detained could call upon an independent judicial authority within 24 hours after that person has been placed in custody in order to be informed of the reasons for detention and place of detention (see Section II of the Memorandum). It also urges the government to make public the charges against and present circumstances of all untried political prisoners who have been held for long periods without trial and to bring them promptly to a fair and open trial or release them.

Amnesty International respectfully recommends that the government considers adopting measures so that any trial procedures relating to political prisoners conform to internationally established norms, particularly with regard to the right to public hearings by an independent and impartial tribunal and the right of the accused to be presumed innocent until proven guilty according to law. It also urges the government to publish detailed records of the trial of all political prisoners. It would particularly appreciate receiving information on a number of recent cases detailed in Section III above.

Amnesty International respectfully recommends that the government considers introducing procedures to ensure the effective protection of prisoners against cruel, inhuman or degrading treatment, in line with the international standards cited in Section IV above. Such procedures should include in particular the right for the family, friends and legal representatives of a person detained to visit the detainee shortly after arrest and regularly thereafter, and to communicate freely with him or her. Amnesty International would welcome information from the appropriate authorities regarding the limitations put upon the detention of prisoners in solitary confinement. It also urges the government to make public the results of investigations in cases where prisoners are reported to have been ill-treated in detention, such as those mentioned in Section IV.

Amnesty International respectfully urges the government to consider taking steps towards the abolition of the death penalty and would welcome information on any measures it might take to reduce the number of offences punishable by the death penalty. It would also welcome information as to the fate of persons sentenced to death with a two-year reprieve whose cases should have come up for review during the past year.

APPENDIX A

Text of article used in evidence
'Democracy or a New Dictatorship'
by Wei Jingsheng
(Abbreviated Translation)

This article by Wei Jingsheng was published in a special issue of the unofficial journal Exploration *in Beijing in March 1979. Wei Jingsheng was arrested shortly after its publication. The article was cited by the prosecution at his trial in October 1979 as one of the writings for which he was accused of "inciting the overthrow of the Dictatorship of the Proletariat" and "carrying out counter-revolutionary agitation and propaganda". The text below is an abbreviated version of the translation of the article by John Scott and Pamela Barnsley which was published in the March 1980 issue of* Harpers and Queen *(London).*

"Everyone in China is well aware that the Chinese social system is not democratic and that this lack of democracy has severely stunted every aspect of the country's social development over the past 30 years. In the face of this hard fact there are two choices before the Chinese people. Either to reform the social system if they want to develop their society and seek a swift increase in the prosperity of their livelihood and economic resources; or, if they are content with a continuation of the Mao Zedong brand of proletarian dictatorship then they cannot even talk of democracy, nor will they be able to realise the modernization of their lives and resources. (. . .)

"Where is China heading and in what sort of society do the people hope to live and work?

"The answer can be seen in the mood of the majority of the people. It is this mood amongst the people that brought about the present democratic movement. With the denial of Mao Zedong's style of dictatorship as its very prerequisite, the aim of this movement is to reform the social system and thereby enable the Chinese people to increase production and develop their lives to the full in a democratic social environment. This aim is not just the aim of a few isolated individuals but represents a whole trend in the development of Chinese society. (. . .) Those who doubt this need only recall the 5 April Movement in 1976, for those who were judged by the court in the minds of the people then, even when they were some of the most powerful in the country have not escaped its ultimate verdict.

"But are there people who remain unafraid of such a judgment? Of course there are—and more than a few of them. Several of those at the top who are drunk with the wielding of power often forget such niceties as the people's judgment, and others out of their personal ambition and despotic inclinations abuse people's credulity. For example, the speech that Vice-

Premier Deng Xiaoping made to leading cadres of the Central Committee on 16 March [1979] was an attempt to take advantage of the people's past confidence in him to oppose the democratic movement itself. He levelled all sorts of charges at the democratic movement and tried to lay on it the blame for the failure of China's production and economy when it was Hua and Deng's political system that was at fault. Thus the people are made the scapegoats for the failure of their leaders' policies. Does Deng Xiaoping really deserve the people's trust? No political leader as an individual has a right to expect the people's unconditional trust. If he carries out policies beneficial to the people along the road to peace and prosperity, then we should trust him. Our trust in him is for his policies and the means to apply these policies. On the other hand, should he carry out policies harmful to the people's interests, the path he is treading is a dictator's path running counter to the people's will, and this should be opposed. The people are as much opposed to this path . . . as they are to measures harmful to their interests and to policies undermining their legitimate rights. According to the principles of democracy any authority must give way to opposition from the people.

"But Deng Xiaoping does not give way. When the people are demanding a widespread inquiry into the reasons for China's backwardness over the last 30 years and into Mao Zedong's crimes against the people, Deng is the first to rush and declare: 'With no Mao Zedong there would be no New China.' Furthermore, in his speech of 16 March [1979] he stubbornly adhered to this and even flattered Mao Zedong's ghost when he called him 'the banner of the Chinese people' and claimed that Mao's weaknesses and mistakes were so insignificant as to be unworthy of mention.

"Is he afraid that an investigation into Mao's mistakes would lead to an investigation into those who were his collaborators? Or is Deng simply preparing to continue the Mao Zedong brand of dictatorial socialist government? If the former is the case, then Deng has nothing to fear, since the tolerance of the Chinese people is great enough to forgive him his past mistakes provided that from now on he leads the country towards democracy and prosperity. But if the latter is the case, we will never forgive him, even if recently he has been the best [of the leaders]. If his aim is to continue the Mao Zedong style of dictatorship, inevitably his course of action could only lead to economic ruin and the abuse of the people's interests. Anyone forgiving such a criminal would himself be indirectly quilty of committing crimes against the people.

"Does Deng Xiaoping want democracy? No, he does not. He is unwilling to comprehend the utter misery of the common people. He is unwilling to allow the people to regain those powers usurped by an ambitious bunch of careerists. He describes the struggle for democratic rights—a movement launched spontaneously by the people—as the actions of troublemakers and of people who want to destroy normal public order which must therefore be repressed. To resort to such measures to deal with people who criticise mistaken policies and with people who demand social development reveals the government's great fear of this popular movement.

"We cannot help asking Mr Deng what his idea of democracy is. If the people have no right to express freely their opinions or to enjoy freedom of speech and criticism, then how can one talk of democracy? If his idea of democracy is a democracy which does not allow others to criticise those in power, then how is such a democracy in the end any different from Mao Zedong's tyranny concealed behind the slogan 'The Democracy of the Dictatorship of the Proletariat'?

"The people want to appeal against injustice, want to vent their grievances, and want democracy, and so they hold meetings. The people oppose famine and dictatorship and so they demonstrate. This clearly shows that without democracy their very livelihood lacks any safeguard. Is it possible, when the people have no power and are so much at the mercy of others . . . that such a situation can be called 'normal public order'? If such 'normal public order' is one that gives to the careerist dictators the right to wreak havoc with the people's interests, then does it benefit the careerists or the people to safeguard such an order? Is the answer not painfully obvious? We consider that normal public order is not total uniformity; particularly in politics, where a normal state of affairs only functions when there exists a great diversity of opinion. When there are no divergent opinions, no diverse discussion and publications, then it is clear that a dictatorship is in existence. Thus, when there is total uniformity, this must surely be called 'abnormal order'. When social phenomena are interpreted as the occasion for criminal elements to make trouble and are used as an excuse to do away with the people's right to express their opinions, this is the time-honoured practice of fascist dictators both new and old. Remember the Tian An Men Square incident, when the Gang of Four used the pretext that certain people had burnt cars as an excuse to crush the popular revolutionary movement. Above all else the people should be forever wary of placing unqualified trust in any one ruler invested with their authority.

"The people should ensure that Deng Xiaoping does not degenerate into a dictator. After he was reinstated in 1975, it seemed he was unwilling to follow Mao Zedong's dictatorial system and would, instead, care for the interests of the people. So the people eagerly looked up to him in the hope that he would realize their aspirations. They were even ready to shed their blood for him—as the Tien An Men Square incident showed. But was such support vested in his person alone? Certainly not. (. . .) If he now wants to discard his mask of protecting the people and take steps to suppress their democratic movement . . . then he certainly does not merit the people's trust and support. From his behaviour it is clear that he is neither concerned with democracy nor does he any longer protect the people's interests. By deceiving the people to win their confidence he is actually following the path to dictatorship.

"It has been demonstrated countless times throughout China's past history that once the confidence of the people has been gained by deception, the dictators work without restraint—for as the ancients said: 'He who can win the people's minds, can win the empire'. Once masters of the whole nation, their private interests inevitably conflict with those of the people, and they must perforce use repression against those very men who are struggling for the interests of the people themselves. So the crux of the matter is not who becomes master of the nation, but rather that . . . the people must maintain a firm control over their own nation, for this is the very essence of democracy. People entrusted with governmental positions . . . must be controlled by the people and be responsible to the people. According to the Constitution of the People's Republic of China organizations and individuals in the administration must be elected by the people, empowered and controlled by an elected government under the supervision of the people and responsible to the people: only then does there exist a legality for executive powers.

"We would like to ask the high officials who instigate the arrest of individuals—is the power you exercise legal or not? We would like to ask Chairman Hua and Vice-Chairman Deng—is your occupation of the highest offices of state based on any form of legality? Further, we would like some elucidation as to why it is the Vice-Chairman and the Vice-Premier and not the courts or organizations representing the people who announce who is to be arrested. Is this state of affairs legal or not?

"And again we would like to ask, according to Chinese law, does the label 'bad element' constitute a criminal per se. In fact by what criterion does one define a 'bad element'? And on whose judgment is such a criterion made? If these simple questions are not clearly answered there is no point in talking about rule by law in China.

"The experience of history tells us that there must be a limit to the amount of trust conferred upon any individual. Anyone seeking the unrestricted and unconditional trust of the people is a man of unbridled ambition. The important problem is to select the right sort of person to put one's trust in, and even more important is how such a person is to be supervised in carrying out the will of the majority. (. . .) We can only trust those representatives who are supervised by us and responsible to us. Moreover such representatives should be chosen by us and not simply thrust upon us. (. . .)

"Only a genuine general election can create a government and leaders ready to serve the interests of the electorate. If the government and its leaders are truly subject to the people's mandate and supervision those two afflictions that leadership is prone to—personal ambition and megalomania—can be avoided. No one should blame leaders for being prone to a touch of power fever. (. . .) Nor should we blame the people for their ignorance in not daring to strike a single blow in their own interests. This may happen because we are without a social system in which a wise people supervises and counterbalances equally sagacious and worthy functionaries.

"Furthering reforms within the social system and moving Chinese politics towards democracy are the prerequisites necessary to solve all the social and economic problems which confront China today. Only by being elected by the people can the leadership gain their voluntary cooperation and bring their initiative into play. Only when the people enjoy complete freedom of expression can they help their leaders to analyse and solve problems . . . Cooperation, together with policies formulated and carried out by the people, are necessary for the highest degree of working efficiency and the achievement of ideal results.

"This is the only road along which present-day China can make progress. Under present-day conditions, it is an extremely difficult path."

APPENDIX B

Criminal Judgment on Xu Wenli by Beijing Municipality Intermediate People's Court

(Translation of a text that appeared in *Baixing,* 16 October 1982)

Prosecutor: Zhang Qisheng, Branch Office of Beijing Municipality People's Procuratorate

Accused: Xu Wenli, also written Xu Wenli [i.e. with different Chinese characters]. Pen-names Xu Shu, Nan Ke, Ke Qing. Male. 38-years-old. From Anqing City in Anhui province. Formerly a worker in the Beijing Construction Section of the Beijing Railways Sub-bureau, living in the Railway Apartments of Andingmen Station in Beijing. Detained on 10 April 1981. Formally arrested for counter-revolutionary crimes on 10 August 1981. Now in custody.

Counsel for
defence: Lawyer Liu Shufen of the Legal Counsel Office of Beijing Municipality

In the counter-revolutionary case against the accused Xu Wenli, brought before the court by the Branch Office of Beijing Municipality People's Procuratorate, this court constituted a judicial panel, according to law, and, with Zhang Qisheng, a procurator from the Branch Office of Beijing Municipality People's Procuratorate, appearing in support of the indictment, has tried the case in open court according to the law. It has now been established.

1. The accused Xu Wenli, in order to overthrow the political power of the people's democratic dictatorship and socialist system of our country, plotted to set up a counter-revolutionary organization, with its leadership mustered from Guangzhou, Qingdao, Anyang and elsewhere by Wang Xizhe, Sun Weibang, Liu Er'an and others (all to be dealt with separately). On three successive evenings from 10 to 12 June 1980, they held secret meetings at the Ganjiakou hotel in Beijing. At the meeting the accused Xu Wenli slandered our people's democratic dictatorship as "a dictatorship of one party". He schemed, by means of "newly developed forms" and "developing a movement nationally", to set up a counter-revolutionary organization, "The Chinese Communist Alliance", and through this "new form of proletarian political party" to "destroy the dictatorship of one party". Wang Xizhe and the others considered that "conditions were not completely ready", they should first "make ideological and organizational preparations". Accordingly, the accused Xu Wenli and the others decided to publish

a "Study Bulletin", whose publication was to be separately carried out by the accused Xu Wenli and Wang Xizhe, Sun Weibang, Xu Shuiliang, Fu Shenqi, Liu Er'an and others in Beijing, Guangzhou, Qingdao, Nanjing, Shanghai, Anyang and elsewhere. Xu Wenli was to serve as overall "manager" from Beijing; he was to be responsible for checking the drafts and the covers and the illustrations. At the same time he/they planned to engage in the process of counter-revolutionary activity by using methods such as creating [favourable] public opinion, seducing and involving people, enmeshing them in their group. From July 1980 until February 1982, altogether six issues of the "Study Bulletin" were published, with several hundred copies of each issue which were circulated to 18 provinces and cities all over China. They openly slandered socialism in our country as "the state capitalism of a privileged bureaucratic autocracy"; they announced such things as "the need to bring about a second revolution", furthering their incitement through counter-revolutionary propaganda.

In order to intensify this counter-revolutionary activity, the accused Xu Wenli set up his signboard of "democratic national construction, peaceful unity" and in the winter of 1980 and spring 1981, separately collaborated with Liu Er'an, Sun Weibang and others, secretly plotting to set up a counter-revolutionary body, the "Chinese Association for the Promotion of Democratic Unity". The accused Xu Wenli wrote a "manifesto" for this counter-revolutionary organization. He also decided to send someone to Hong Kong and other places to engage in collaboration with anti-China anti-communist elements. Furthermore, he himself wrote a letter to anti-China anti-communist elements in Hong Kong, elaborated his tactics and plan of action to set up a "Chinese Association for the Promotion of Democracy", plotting to establish the general office of this counter-revolutionary organization in Hong Kong, with "four sub-sections for the Mainland, Taiwan, Hong Kong and Overseas" and with "other areas setting up branch organizations". Thus Hong Kong would be a "bridge" for collaboration between anti-China anti-communist elements; "a suitable opportunity would be chosen to hold an absolutely secret delegates conference, either in Hong Kong or overseas". He plotted to make this counter-revolutionary organization into a "resilient and undefeatable political entity", with what he called "real power", which would "force the Communist Party to give way", would "organize a provisional government", would "hold a general election" and "compose a new government", overthrowing the power of the people's democratic dictatorship in our country.

2. On 29 March 1979 Beijing Municipal Revolutionary Committee issued a "decree" on maintaining social order in the capital. The accused Xu Wenli subsequently, from April to August 1979, distributed leaflets at the "Xidan wall", defaming the "decree" as "the use of violent oppression", "the strangulation of democracy", inciting the masses to resist the implementation of a government law. The accused Xu Wenli also carried out what he called "a test of the people's will", made speeches, wrote essays, put up posters and distributed leaflets; he distorted the real situation, reversed black and white, and incited the masses; he opposed the legal authorities in their

just decisions on counter-revolutionary elements and their correct handling of law-breaking criminals; he sent essays vilifying the legal authorities to foreign reporters and foreign ambassadors in China; he used the postal service and deliveries to disseminate his writings abroad, to cheat public opinion and mislead the public; this was a pretext for the attacks and slander of anti-China anti-communist elements. In the articles there were slanders and lies; they slandered our country as being "strangulating feudal socialism". They openly called for the reform of China's social system, carrying out incitement through counter-revolutionary propaganda.

In regard to the crimes mentioned above, there is witness testimony. The statements of the co-defendants, the technical appraisal and the resulting testimony provide the evidence of the case. The true facts are clear, the evidence is complete and reliable enough to be certain.

This court considers that the accused Xu Wenli, as the leader of a group of people, plotted and schemed to organize a counter-revolution clique, actively engaged in counter-revolutionary activity, created false slanders, carried out counter-revolutionary propaganda, incited the masses to defy and sabotage the implementation of the decrees and laws of the state, plotted to overthrow the political power of the people's democratic dictatorship and the socialist system in China; the offences of having organized a counter-revolutionary clique and of having engaged in incitement through counter-revolutionary propaganda have been established; the circumstances of the case are serious; a severe penalty is required. In order to strengthen the people's democratic dictatorship and the socialist system in our country, to punish counter-revolutionary elements who threaten the security of the state and social order, according to the provisions of Articles 90, 98, 102, 52, 51 (1), 64, 60 of the "Criminal Law of the People's Republic of China", the judgment is as follows:

1. The accused Xu Wenli, guilty of organizing a counter-revolutionary clique, is sentenced to imprisonment for a fixed term of 12 years and deprivation of political rights for three years. For the crime of counter-revolutionary propaganda and agitation, he is sentenced to a fixed term of five years' imprisonment and deprivation of political rights for two years. It is decided that he must serve a fixed term of 15 years' imprisonment, with four years' deprivation of political rights. (The period of the sentence is to be counted from the date of execution of the judgment; as for the period of detention before the announcement of the judgment, each day shall count as one day of the carrying out of the sentence.)

2. The material evidence which was seized is confiscated (an inventory is attached).

If the decision of this court is not accepted, from the day after this decision of the court is received and within 10 days, the defendant may ask this court for a petition of appeal and appeal to the High People's Court of Beijing Municipality.

Chief Justice: Ding Fengchun

People's Assessor: Bi Jiali

People's Assessor: Zhang Congliang
8 June 1982
Clerk: Shi Xuechen

This document has been checked against the original and there are no discrepancies.

Intermediate People's Court of Beijing Municipality

List of confiscated goods

1. One printing machine
2. Four steel (stencil?) boards
3. Three charts
4. One box of duplicating paper
5. Two rolls of paper
6. A bundle of manuscripts
7. A bundle of magazines
8. 8 copies of "Gangkan" magazine
9. 5 copies of "Zhongbao Monthly"
10. 10 copies of "Zhengming"
11. 4 copies of "Beidou"
12. 5 copies of "Guangjiaojing"
13. 20 copies of "Observer Monthly"
14. 3 bound volumes of "Observer Monthly"
15. 5 copies of "Mingbao Monthly"
16. 4 copies of "Jingbao"
17. 18 copies of "Seventies"
18. One copy of "Memorial volume on Tiananmen incident"
19. 14 copies of "Zhongguoren"
20. 12 copies of "Nanbeiji"
21. 13 copies of "Zhangwang"
22. 16 copies of "Dongxiang"
23. 2 copies of "Haiding Magazine"
24. One volume of speeches by Wang Xizhe
25. One copy of "New Society"
26. One copy of "Left-wing Review"
27. One copy of "Collected underground journals from the Mainland"
28. One copy of "Between Hong Kong and China"
29. One copy of "18 years of struggle"
30. 3 copies of "Huanghe"
31. 2 copies of "Dongxifang"
32. 6 volumes of "Spring and Autumn Annals"
33. 4 volumes of "Shidai Zhonkan"

34. One copy of "Science and Engineering Students Paper"
35. One copy of "Study Bulletin"
36. One copy of "What is to be done?"
37. One copy of "Saving the Seeds"
38. 5 copies of "Dangdai"
39. 19 copies of notebooks
40. 21 reels of tape recordings

APPENDIX C

Offences Punishable by the Death Penalty in the People's Republic of China

I   According to the Criminal Law as effective on 1 January 1980:

a)   The Criminal Law lists 14 "counter-revolutionary" (i.e. political) offences which may be punished by death if they are "of a particularly heinous nature causing great harm to the people and the state" (Article 103). They are listed in nine articles as follows:

Article 91
Offenders colluding with foreign countries and conspiring to jeopardize the sovereignty, territorial integrity and security of the motherland will be sentenced to life imprisonment or fixed-term imprisonment of not less than 10 years.

Article 92
Those plotting to overthrow the government and split the country will be sentenced to life imprisonment or fixed-term imprisonment of not less than 10 years.

Article 93
Those instigating, seducing or bribing any state functionary or any member of the Armed Forces, the People's Police or the Militia to defect, turn traitor or rebel will be sentenced to life imprisonment or fixed-term imprisonment of not less than 10 years.

Article 94
Those defecting and turning traitor will be sentenced to fixed-term imprisonment of not less than three and not more than 10 years. Those guilty of serious cases of defecting and turning traitor or who lead their men to defect to the enemy and turn traitor, will be sentenced to imprisonment of not less than 10 years or life imprisonment.

Article 95
Major culprits of armed rebellious assemblies or other serious offences will be sentenced to life imprisonment or fixed-term imprisonment of not less than 10 years. Those taking an active part will be sentenced to fixed-term imprisonment of not less than three and not more than 10 years.

Article 96
Major culprits gathering a mob to storm prisons and release prisoners or organizing jailbreaks or other serious offences will be sentenced to fixed-term imprisonment of not less than 10 years. Those taking an active part

will be sentenced to fixed-term imprisonment of not less than three and not more than 10 years.

Article 97

Those committing espionage or supporting the enemy in the following manner will be sentenced to imprisonment of not less than 10 years, or life imprisonment. In less serious cases, they will be sentenced to fixed-term imprisonment of not less than three and not more than 10 years: (1) Stealing, spying and supplying information to the enemy; (2) Supplying arms or other military materials to the enemy; and (3) Joining a secret service or espionage organization or receiving orders from the enemy.

Article 100

Any of the following destructive acts for counter-revolutionary purposes will be punishable by life imprisonment or fixed-term imprisonment of not less than 10 years. In less serious cases they will be sentenced to fixed-term imprisonment of not less than three and not more than 10 years.

(1) Destruction or damage to any military installation, production facility, telecommunications and transportation installation, building project and safety installation or other public building and property through explosion, arson or deliberate inundation; (2) Theft of any state document or military material and robbing of any factory and mining expertise, bank, department store, warehouse or other public property; (3) Highjacking of any ship, aircraft, train, trolley, or motor car; (4) Directing the enemy to any bombing or shelling target; and (5) Making, robbing or stealing any gun or ammunition.

Article 101

The use of poison, bacteria and other methods to kill and injure people for counter-revolutionary purposes will be punishable by life imprisonment or fixed-term imprisonment of not less than 10 years. Less serious cases will be sentenced to fixed-term imprisonment of not less than three and not more than 10 years.

b)   Offences dealing with violation of public security:

Article 106

Any act of arson, deliberate dam sabotages, explosion, use of poison or other dangerous methods resulting in serious injury and death and causing great loss to public property will be punishable by fixed-term imprisonment of not less than 10 years, life imprisonment or the death penalty.

Article 110

Any act of sabotage to means of transportation, transportation installation, electric power and gas installations and flammable and explosive installations resulting in serious accident will be punishable by fixed-term imprisonment of not less than 10 years, life imprisonment or the death penalty. Unpremeditated offences as above will be punishable by fixed-term imprisonment or detention of not more than seven years.

c)   Acts against a citizen's personal and democratic rights:

Article 132

Anyone who commits deliberate homicide will be sentenced to death, life imprisonment or imprisonment for not less than 10 years. In minor cases, the offender will be sentenced to imprisonment for not less than three years and not more than 10 years.

Article 137

It is strictly forbidden to gather a crowd for "beating, smashing and looting". If someone is disabled or killed, whoever gathers a crowd for "beating, smashing and looting" will be charged with injury and murder. In case public or private property is damaged or robbed, the major culprit will be charged with robbery and ordered to return what he has unlawfully taken or pay compensation for it. Whoever commits the aforesaid offence may be exclusively deprived of political rights.

Article 139

Anyone who commits rape by force, threats or other means will be sentenced to imprisonment for not less than three years and no more than 10. Anyone who seduces a female minor under 14 years of age will be charged with rape and severely punished. In particularly grave cases or where the victim is seriously wounded or killed, a person who commits either one of the aforesaid offences will be sentenced to death, life imprisonment or imprisonment for not less than 10 years. Two or more persons who commit rape and violate the same victim will in turn be severely punished.

d) Encroachment on property:

Article 150

Anyone who steals public or private property by force, threats or other means will be sentenced to imprisonment for not less than three years and no more than 10. Anyone who commits the aforesaid offence and the circumstances are grave or someone is seriously injured or killed may be sentenced to imprisonment for not less than 10 years, life imprisonment or death. At the same time, his property may be confiscated.

Article 155

A state functionary who takes advantage of his position and power to embezzle public property will be sentenced to detention or imprisonment for not more than five years. In grave cases where the amount involved is huge, the offender will be sentenced to imprisonment for not less than five years. In extremely grave cases, the offender will be sentenced to life imprisonment or death. Anyone who is guilty of the aforesaid offence will concurrently have his property confiscated or be ordered to return what he has unlawfully taken or pay compensation for it. Personnel entrusted by state organs, enterprises, business units or mass organizations to perform public duties who commit the first category of offence mentioned above will be punished according to the first two categories.

*II   On 10 June 1981, the Standing Committee of the
National People's Congress adopted the "Provisional
Regulations of the PRC on Punishing Servicemen who
Commit Offences Against Their Duties", which list the
following offences as liable to the death penalty. The
regulations became effective on 1 January 1982:*

Article 4

. . . Any person who steals, collects or furnishes military secrets to enemies
or foreigners may be sentenced to fixed-term imprisonment of not less than
10 years, life imprisonment or death.

Article 10

Any person who resorts to violence or threats to obstruct command personnel
on shift or station duty from performing their duties may be sentenced to
fixed-term imprisonment of not more than five years or detention at hard
labour, and in serious cases to fixed-term imprisonment of not less than five
years. In especially serious cases or in cases of serious injuries or deaths
resulting from such offences, offenders may be sentenced to life imprisonment or death. During wartime, the punishment may be more severe.

Article 11

In cases of theft of weapons, equipment or military supplies, offenders may
be sentenced to fixed-term imprisonment of not more than five years or
detention at hard labour, and in serious cases, to fixed-term imprisonment
of not less than five years and not more than 10 years. In especially serious
cases, offenders may be sentenced to fixed-term imprisonment of not less
than 10 years or life imprisonment. During wartime, the punishment may
be more severe, and offenders may be given the death sentence if the offences
are especially serious.

Article 12

Any person who commits the crime of sabotaging weapons, equipment or
military installations may be sentenced to fixed-term imprisonment of not
more than three years or detention at hard labour. In cases of sabotage of
major weapons, equipment or military installations, offenders may be sentenced to fixed-term imprisonment of not less than three years and not
more than 10 years. In especially serious cases, offenders may be sentenced
to fixed-term imprisonment of not less than 10 years, life imprisonment or
death. During wartime, the punishment may be more severe.

Article 14

Any person who fabricates rumours to mislead others and undermine army
morale during wartime may be sentenced to fixed-term imprisonment of
not more than three years, and in serious cases to fixed-term imprisonment
of not less than three years but not more than 10 years. Any person who
colludes with the enemy to spread rumours so as to mislead others and
undermine army morale may be sentenced to fixed-term imprisonment of
not less than 10 years or life imprisonment. In especially serious cases,
offenders may be given the death sentence.

Article 16

All servicemen who showed cowardice and desert from the battlefield will be sentenced to three years' imprisonment or less; in serious cases, they will be sentenced to three to 10 years' imprisonment; and in cases which resulted in major losses in battle or war, they will be sentenced to 10 years to life imprisonment or death.

Article 17

All servicemen who disobey orders during a battle, thus jeopardizing the outcome of a war, will be sentenced to three to 10 years' imprisonment, and in cases of serious harm to the battle or war effort they will be sentenced to 10 years to life imprisonment or death.

Article 18

All servicemen who intentionally make false reports about the military situation and fake military orders, thus jeopardizing military operations, will be sentenced to three to 10 years' imprisonment, and in cases of serious harm to the battle and war effort they will be sentenced to 10 years to life imprisonment or death.

Article 19

All servicemen who are afraid of death in battle and voluntarily lay down weapons and surrender to the enemy will be sentenced to three to 10 years' imprisonment, and in cases of a serious nature they will be sentenced to 10 years to life imprisonment. All servicemen who, after surrendering to the enemy, assist the enemy will be sentenced to 10 years to life imprisonment or death.

Article 20

All servicemen who plunder and harm innocent residents in military operational areas will be sentenced to seven years or less; in serious cases, they will be sentenced to more than seven years' imprisonment; and in cases of a particularly serious nature, they will be sentenced to life imprisonment or death.

III The following offences listed in the Criminal Law became liable to the death penalty when the National People's Congress Standing Committee adopted amendments to the Criminal Law in April 1982. When these amendments were adopted, it was specified that the cases which might be punished by the death penalty were "particularly grave cases":

Article 118

Those who make a regular business of smuggling, speculating and profiteering, engage in smuggling, speculating and profiteering in a big way or are ringleaders in smuggling, speculating and profiteering groups will be sentenced to fixed-term imprisonment of not less than three and not more than 10 years. They can concurrently be sentenced to the confiscation of property.

Article 119
State functionaries who take advantage of their position to engage in smuggling, speculating and profiteering will be severely punished.

Article 152
A habitual thief or swindler or anyone who takes a huge amount of public or private property by stealing, swindling or plundering will be sentenced to imprisonment for not less than five and not more than 10 years. In extremely grave cases, the offender will be sentenced to imprisonment for not less than 10 years or life and may at the same time have his property confiscated.

Article 171
Anyone who manufactures, sells or ships opium, heroin, morphine or other narcotic drugs will be sentenced to detention or imprisonment for not more than five years; a fine may be imposed concurrently. Anyone who manufactures, sells or ships the aforementioned narcotics persistently or in bulk will be sentenced to imprisonment for not less than five years; a fine may be imposed concurrently or exclusively.

Article 173
Anyone who steals or exports valuable cultural relics in violation of relics protection regulations will be sentenced to imprisonment for not less than three years and no more than 10; a fine may be imposed concurrently. In grave cases, the offender may be sentenced to life imprisonment or imprisonment for not less than 10 years; his property may be confiscated concurrently.

Article 185
Any state functionary who exploits his office and takes bribes will be sentenced to detention or imprisonment for not more than five years. Money or goods received in bribes will be confiscated and steps will be taken to recover public funds or property that have been illegally taken away.

IV   The following offences listed in the Criminal Law became liable to the death penalty when the National People's Congress Standing Committee adopted amendments to the Criminal Law in September 1983.

(These amendments were recorded in "The Decision of the NPC Standing Committee on Severely Punishing Criminals who gravely endanger public security".) The cases liable to the death penalty were those considered "particularly grave":

Article 99
Those organizing and utilizing feudal superstitious beliefs, secret societies or sects to carry out counter-revolutionary activities will be sentenced to fixed-term imprisonment of not less than five years. In less serious cases they will be sentenced to fixed-term imprisonment, detention, surveillance or deprivation of political rights for not more than five years.

Article 112
The illegal making, trading and transporting of arms and ammunition or the theft in any form of guns and ammunition from state organs, police or

militiamen will be punishable by fixed-term imprisonment of not more than seven years. In serious cases this will be punishable by fixed-term imprisonment of not less than seven years or life imprisonment.

Article 134

Anyone who commits deliberate assault and battery will be sentenced to detention or imprisonment for not more than three years. Whoever commits the aforesaid offence and causes severe injury to another person will be sentenced to imprisonment for not less than three years and no more than seven years; if he causes death to another person, he will be sentenced to life imprisonment or not less than seven years. Where separate provisions are laid down in the present law, such provisions will be followed.

Article 140

Anyone who forces a female to engage in prostitution will be sentenced to imprisonment for not less than three years and no more than 10.

Article 141

Anyone who engages in abduction for purposes of trafficking in human beings will be sentenced to imprisonment for not more than five years. In grave cases, the offender will be sentenced to imprisonment for not less than five years.

Article 160

In vile cases, anyone who incites group fighting, creates disturbances, subjects women to indignities or carries out other gangster activities to disrupt public order will be sentenced to imprisonment for not more than seven years, detention or surveillance. The ringleader of a criminal gang will be sentenced to imprisonment for not less than seven years.

Article 169

Anyone who lures or houses a female and makes her engage in prostitution for the purpose of seeking profits will be sentenced to imprisonment for not more than five years, detention or surveillance. In grave cases, the offender will be sentenced to imprisonment for not less than five years; a fine may be imposed or property confiscated concurrently.

The NPC decision also provided the death penalty for people who "pass on methods of committing crimes" in the following terms:

> "In a serious case, the offender shall be sentenced to imprisonment for not less than five years and in a particularly grave case, the offender will be sentenced to life imprisonment or death."

This clause may therefore apply to Article 26 of the Criminal Law which reads as follows:

Article 26

A person who instigates others to commit crimes should be punished according to the role he plays in the joint offence. A person who instigates a person under 18 years old to commit a crime should be severely punished. If the instigated person has not actually committed the crime, the instigator may be give a lighter or mitigated penalty.

APPENDIX D

Articles of the International Covenant on Civil and Political Rights

Article 6

1. Every human being has the inherent right to life. This right shall be protected by law. No one shall be arbitrarily deprived of his life.

2. In countries which have not abolished the death penalty, sentence of death may be imposed only for the most serious crimes in accordance with the law in force at the time of the commission of the crime and not contrary to the provisions of the present Covenant and to the Convention on the Prevention and Punishment of the Crime of Genocide. This penalty can only be carried out pursuant to a final judgement rendered by a competent court.

3. When deprivation of life constitutes the crime of genocide, it is understood that nothing in this article shall authorize any State Party to the present Covenant to derogate in any way from any obligation assumed under the provisions of the Convention on the Prevention and Punishment of the Crime of Genocide.

4. Anyone sentenced to death shall have the right to seek pardon or commutation of the sentence. Amnesty, pardon or commutation of the sentence of death may be granted in all cases.

5. Sentence of death shall not be imposed for crimes committed by persons below eighteen years of age and shall not be carried out on pregnant women.

6. Nothing in this article shall be invoked to delay or prevent the abolition of capital punishment by any State Party to the present Covenant.

Article 14

1. All persons shall be equal before the courts and tribunals. In the determination of any criminal charge against him, or of his rights and obligations in a suit at law, everyone shall be entitled to a fair and public hearing by a competent, independent and impartial tribunal established by law. The Press and the public may be excluded from all or part of a trial for reasons of morals, public order *(ordre public)* or national security in a democratic society, or when the interest of the private lives of the parties so requires, or to the extent strictly necessary in the opinion of the court in special circumstances where publicity would prejudice the interests of justice; but any judgement rendered in a criminal case or in a suit at law shall be made public except where the interests of juvenile persons otherwise requires or the proceedings concern matrimonial disputes or the guardianship of children.

2. Everyone charged with a criminal offence shall have the right to be presumed innocent until proved guilty according to law.

3. In the determination of any criminal charge against him, everyone shall be entitled to the following minimum guarantees, in full equality:

(a) To be informed promptly and in detail in a language which he understands of the nature and cause of the charge against him;

(b) To have adequate time and facilities for the preparation of his defence and to communicate with counsel of his own choosing;

(c) To be tried without undue delay;

(d) To be tried in his presence, and to defend himself in person or through legal assistance of his own choosing; to be informed, if he does not have legal assistance, of this right; and to have legal assistance assigned to him, in any case where the interests of justice so require, and without payment by him in any such case if he does not have sufficient means to pay for it;

(e) To examine, or have examined, the witnesses against him and to obtain the attendance and examination of witnesses on his behalf under the same conditions as witnesses against him;

(f) To have the free assistance of an interpreter if he cannot understand or speak the language used in court;

(g) Not to be compelled to testify against himself or to confess guilt.

4. In the case of juvenile persons, the procedure shall be such as will take account of their age and the desirability of promoting their rehabilitation.

5. Everyone convicted of a crime shall have the right to his conviction and sentence being reviewed by a higher tribunal according to law.

6. When a person has by a final decision been convicted of a criminal offence and when subsequently his conviction has been reversed or he has been pardoned on the ground that a new or newly discovered fact shows conclusively that there has been a miscarriage of justice, the person who has suffered punishment as a result of such conviction shall be compensated according to law, unless it is proved that the non-disclosure of the unknown fact in time is wholly or partly attributable to him.

7. No one shall be liable to be tried or punished again for an offence for which he has already been finally convicted or acquitted in accordance with the law and penal procedure of each country.

Article 15

1. No one shall be held guilty of any criminal offence on account of any act or omission which did not constitute a criminal offence, under national or international law, at the time when it was committed. Nor shall a heavier penalty be imposed than the one that was applicable at the time when the criminal offence was committed. If, subsequent to the commission of the offence, provision is made by law for the imposition of a lighter penalty, the offender shall benefit thereby.

2. Nothing in this article shall prejudice the trial and punishment of any person for any act or omission which, at the time when it was committed, was criminal according to the general principles of law recognized by the community of nations.

Copies of the complete text of the International Covenant on Civil and Political Rights are available from local United Nations information offices.

Amnesty International — a worldwide campaign

In recent years, people throughout the world have become more and more aware of the urgent need to protect human rights effectively in every part of the world.

• Countless men and women are in prison for their beliefs. They are being held as prisoners of conscience in scores of countries—in crowded jails, in labour camps and in remote prisons.

• Thousands of political prisoners are being held under administrative detention orders and denied any possibility of a trial or an appeal.

• Others are forcibly confined in psychiatric hospitals or secret detention camps.

• Many are forced to endure relentless, systematic torture.

• More than a hundred countries retain the death penalty.

• Political leaders and ordinary citizens are becoming the victims of abductions, "disappearances" and killings, carried out both by government forces and opposition groups.

An international effort

To end secret arrests, torture and killing requires organized and worldwide effort. Amnesty International is part of that effort.

Launched as an independent organization over 20 years ago, Amnesty International is open to anyone prepared to work universally for the release of prisoners of conscience, for fair trials for political prisoners and for an end to torture and executions.

The movement now has members and supporters in more than 160 countries. It is independent of any government, political group, ideology, economic interest or religious creed.

It began with a newspaper article, "The Forgotten Prisoners", published on 28 May 1961 in *The Observer* (London) and reported in *Le Monde* (Paris).

Announcing an impartial campaign to help victims of political persecution, the British lawyer Peter Benenson wrote:

Open your newspaper any day of the week and you will find a report from somewhere in the world of someone being imprisoned, tortured or executed because his opinions or religion are unacceptable to his government. . . . The newspaper reader feels a sickening sense of impotence. Yet if these feelings of disgust all over the world could be united into common action, something effective could be done.

Within a week he had received more than a thousand offers of support—to collect information, publicize it and approach governments. The groundwork was laid for a permanent human rights organization that eventually became known as Amnesty International. The first chairperson of its International Executive Committee (from 1963 to 1974) was Sean MacBride, who received the Nobel Peace Prize in 1974 and the Lenin Prize in 1975.

The mandate

Amnesty International is playing a specific role in the international protection of human rights.

It seeks the *release* of men and women detained anywhere because of their beliefs, colour, sex, ethnic origin, language or religious creed, provided they have not used or advocated violence. These are termed *prisoners of conscience*.

It works for *fair and prompt trials* for *all political prisoners* and works on behalf of such people detained without charge or trial.

It opposes the *death penalty* and *torture* or other cruel, inhuman or degrading treatment or punishment of *all prisoners* without reservation.

Amnesty International acts on the basis of the Universal Declaration of Human Rights and other international convenants. Amnesty International is convinced of the indivisibility and mutual dependence of all human rights. Through the practical work for prisoners within its mandate, Amnesty International participates in the wider promotion and protection of human rights in the civil, political, economic, social and cultural spheres.

Amnesty International does not oppose or support any government or political system. Its members around the world include supporters of differing systems who agree on the defence of all people in all countries against imprisonment for their beliefs, and against torture and execution.

Amnesty International at work

The working methods of Amnesty International are based on the principle of international responsibility for the protection of human rights. The movement tries to take action wherever and whenever there are violations of those human rights falling within its mandate. Since it was founded, Amnesty International groups have intervened on behalf of more than 25,000 prisoners in over a hundred countries with widely differing ideologies.

A unique aspect of the work of Amnesty International groups—placing the emphasis on the need for *international* human rights work—is the fact that each group works on behalf of prisoners held in countries other than its own. At least two prisoner cases are assigned to each group; the cases are balanced geographically and politically to ensure impartiality.

There are now 3,341 local Amnesty International groups throughout the world. There are sections in 43 countries (in Africa, Asia, the Americas, Europe and the Middle East) and individual members, subscribers and supporters in more than 120 other countries. Members do not work on cases in their own countries. No section, group or member is expected to provide information on their own country and no section, group or member has any responsibility for action taken or statements issued by the international organization concerning their own country.

Continuous research

The movement attaches the highest importance to balanced and accurate reporting of facts. All its activities depend on meticulous research into allegations of human rights violations. The International Secretariat in London (with a staff of 175, comprising 30 nationalities) has a Research Department which collects and analyses information from a wide variety of sources. These include hundreds of newspapers and journals, government bulletins, transcriptions of radio broadcasts, reports from lawyers and humanitarian organizations, as well as letters from prisoners and their families. Amnesty International also sends fact-finding missions for on-the-spot investigations and to observe trials, meet prisoners and interview government officials. Amnesty International takes full responsibility for its published reports and if proved wrong on any point is prepared to issue a correction.

Once the relevant facts are established, information is sent to sections and groups for action. The members then start the work of trying to protect the individuals whose human rights are reported to have been violated. They send letters to government ministers and embassies. They organize public meetings, arrange special publicity events, such as vigils at appropriate government offices or embassies, and try to interest newspapers in the cases they have taken up. They ask their friends and colleagues to help in the effort. They collect signatures for international petitions and raise money to send relief, such as medicine, food and clothing, to the prisoners and their families.

A permanent campaign

Symbol of
Amnesty International

In addition to case work on behalf of individual prisoners, Amnesty International members campaign for the abolition of torture and the death penalty. This includes trying to prevent torture and executions when people have been taken to known torture centres or sentenced to death. Volunteers in dozens of countries can be alerted in such cases, and within hours hundreds of telegrams and other appeals can be on their way to the government, prison or detention centre.

Amnesty International condemns as a matter of principle the torture and execution of prisoners by *anyone*, including opposition groups. Governments have the responsibility of dealing with such abuses, acting in conformity with international standards for the protection of human rights.

In its efforts to mobilize world public opinion, Amnesty International neither supports nor opposes economic or cultural boycotts. It *does* take a stand against the international transfer of military, police or security equipment and expertise likely to be used by recipient governments to detain prisoners of conscience and to inflict torture and carry out executions.

Amnesty International does not grade governments or countries according to their record on human rights. Not only does repression in various countries prevent the free flow of information about human rights abuses, but the techniques of repression and their impact vary widely. Instead of attempting comparisons, Amnesty International concentrates on trying to end the specific violations of human rights in each case.

Policy and funds

Amnesty International is a democratically run movement. Every two years major policy decisions are taken by an International Council comprising representatives from all the sections. They elect an International Executive Committee to carry out their decisions and supervise the day-to-day running of the International Secretariat.

The organization is financed by its members throughout the world, by individual subscriptions and donations. Members pay fees and conduct fund-raising campaigns—they organize concerts and art auctions and are often to be seen on fund-raising drives at street corners in their neighbourhoods.

Its rules about accepting donations are strict and ensure that any funds received by any part of the organization do not compromise it in any way, affect its integrity, make it dependent on any donor, or limit its freedom of activity.

The organization's accounts are audited annually and are published with its annual report.

Amnesty International has formal relations with the United Nations (ECOSOC), UNESCO, the Council of Europe, the Organization of African Unity and the Organization of American States.

How to subscribe to Amnesty International

A subscription to Amnesty International will give you access to new—often unpublished—information about human rights abuses on a global, independent and impartial basis. By subscribing to Amnesty International you will also receive details about how you can help the people who are the victims.

Amnesty International Newsletter

This monthly bulletin is a regular update on Amnesty International's work: reports of fact-finding missions, details about political prisoners, reliable reports of torture and executions. It is written—without political bias—for human rights activists throughout the world and is widely used by journalists, students, political leaders, medical doctors, lawyers and other professionals.

Amnesty International Report

This annual report is a country-by-country survey of Amnesty International's work to combat political imprisonment, torture and the death penalty throughout the world. The report is organized into sections and normally covers at least 100 countries. It is probably the most widely read—and most influential—of the many reports published by Amnesty International each year.

Annual newsletter subscription: 5.00 (US$12.50)
Subscription to both the newsletter and report:
10.00 (US$25.00)

Amnesty International Publications Catalogue

The Amnesty International publications catalogue lists all recent major Amnesty International reports and documents, together with a selection of earlier publications still in print. It is available, free of charge, from Amnesty International Publications.

Write to: **Amnesty International Publications, 1 Easton Street, London WC1X 8DJ, United Kingdom,** or your local section.